ClarisVvorks
for Windows

More Software Application Tutorials from McGraw-Hill

ClarisWorks for Windows

FRITZ J. ERICKSON
Millersville University of Pennsylvania

JOHN A. VONK
University of Northern Colorado

 McGRAW-HILL

New York St. Louis San Francisco Auckland Bogotá
Caracas Lisbon London Madrid Mexico Milan Montreal
New Delhi Paris San Juan Singapore Sydney Tokyo Toronto

McGraw-Hill

ClarisWorks for Windows

Copyright © 1994 by **McGraw-Hill, Inc**. All rights reserved.
Printed in the United States of America. Except as permitted under
the United States Copyright Act of 1976, no part of this publication
may be reproduced or distributed in any form or by any means, or
stored in a database or retieval system, without the prior written
permission of the publisher.

1 2 3 4 5 6 7 8 9 0   SEM SEM   9 0 9 8 7 6 5 4

ISBN 0-07-021244-9

Sponsoring editor: Dean Barton
Production supervisor: Richard DeVitto
Project manager: Graphics West
Interior designer: Graphics West
Cover designer: Tom Trujillo
Printer and binder: Semline, Inc.

Library of Congress Card Catalog No. 94-75033

Table of Contents

Preface

ClarisWorks for Windows may be the only piece of software you will ever truly need. Of course, there are some games you might want to play. Maybe there is an accounting package or check-writing program needed. There may even be instructional programs that are of some use. But for the majority of uses, ClarisWorks for Windows provides all the tools needed by most computer users.

The reason ClarisWorks for Windows may be the only program you will ever need is simple—ClarisWorks for Windows is an integrated software package. *Integrated* means that ClarisWorks for Windows is a collection of the most popular types of computer applications all bundled into one easy-to-use, easy-to-operate, easy-to-learn package. ClarisWorks for Windows is a word processor, a spreadsheet, a database, a graphics program, and even a telecommunications system.

There are other integrated computer packages available. So why choose ClarisWorks for Windows? For many, the answer is that ClarisWorks for Windows is so easy to learn and use, yet provides such a strong feature set that there may be no reason to learn any other. As some say, why not learn the best, and forget the rest?

This book is dedicated to helping you learn to use ClarisWorks for Windows quickly and efficiently. We do this by following some basic, yet important principles of learning.

First, we all learn best if we know why we are learning. With this book, every chapter begins with an overview of what you will learn and what you can expect to accomplish. This is done in the Overview sections as well as through a precise Objectives list.

Second, we learn best if we can anticipate the outcome. Each section within the book explains what can be accomplished and how ClarisWorks for Windows can help accomplish the task.

Third, we learn best if we apply our new-found knowledge. Throughout each chapter are several Hands-On sections. Each section is designed to provide you with a guided tutorial for learning specific components of ClarisWorks for Windows. With this structure, you can read what, and why, and then apply.

Finally, learning occurs best when you can review what you have learned and apply that knowledge to new situations. Every chapter ends with a detailed summary, questions, and a quiz to reinforce your new knowledge. Each chapter also contains exercises, some interspersed through the chapter, some at chapter end. The exercises help you better understand how the different applications within ClarisWorks for Windows can help you solve problems.

We hope you have as much fun learning about ClarisWorks for Windows as we did writing this text. We are certain you will find ClarisWorks for Windows a productive tool.

Acknowledgements

We were very fortunate to have capable, professional people provide reviews and make helpful comments at numerous stages in the development of this text. We thank our reviewers J. Steven Soulier from Utah State University, James H. Wiebe at the California State University at Los Angeles, and Christine Swarm with Northeastern Illinois University. We are also indebted to our many colleagues and students for their insight and inspiration. Most notably we would like to thank Troy Isaak for his thoughtful suggestions and for acting as a sounding board. Finally, we are also most grateful to our friends at McGraw-Hill.

Welcome home John Andres.

To Gordon Smith: A friend for all seasons.

MICROSOFT WINDOWS ESSENTIALS

OBJECTIVES

Learning the material in this chapter will enable you to:

- define the purpose of Microsoft Windows
- use a mouse to control Windows
- use pull-down menus
- identify different types of icons
- identify and use components of a window
- use multiple windows
- control dialog boxes

OVERVIEW

If you are not familiar with Microsoft Windows, this chapter is for you. If you are comfortable using Microsoft Windows, then you may want to give this chapter a brief review. Either way, this chapter will not make you a Windows expert. It will, however, start you in the right direction.

MICROSOFT WINDOWS

Learning to use any computer begins with understanding the set of controlling commands that directs the entire computer system. For the IBM and IBM compatible family of computers, the dominant operating system is DOS, an acronym for Disk Operating System. There are two available versions of DOS—MS-DOS (Microsoft DOS) and PC-DOS (Personal Computer DOS). Both versions are very similar; the only major difference is the distributor. MS-DOS was developed by Microsoft for use with computers that operate much like IBM computers (known as IBM compatibles). PC-DOS is distributed by IBM primarily for IBM brand computers. Because both function the same, most users simply say "DOS" when referring to either MS- or PC-DOS.

DOS is a command-driven operating system. To use DOS, you must type specific and detailed commands, then press the Enter key. For example, if you want to copy a file from one location to another, you might type COPY C:\WORLD\HISTORY\US\CIVIL.WAR E:\TRANSFER\CIVIL.TMP. If you want to execute a word processing program, you might type something like the following:

C: [Enter]

CD \WP\PROG [Enter]

C:\WP\PROG\WP [Enter]

It seems simple—type a command and press Enter. Unfortunately, if you are not familiar with DOS, the three previous lines may as well be in a foreign language. Learning the commands and the command structure can be one of the most frustrating experiences for new computer users. While DOS is very powerful, it has a long-standing reputation for being difficult to learn and use. For this reason, some software manufacturers have developed programs designed to make DOS easier. Instead of replacing DOS, these programs offer enhancements to simplify the learning process and, more importantly, to ease the controlling of a DOS-based computer. Microsoft Windows (Windows for short) is just such a program.

Microsoft Windows is a graphical user interface (GUI) that automates many of the functions of DOS. Using icons (pictures), menus, and a mouse, Microsoft Windows controls the computer without having to deal exclusively with DOS commands. Instead of learning to use all of DOS' command structure, you need only learn to control the computer by pointing at objects on the screen and clicking a mouse button. In short, Microsoft Windows makes using a DOS-based computer much easier and more efficient.

The Windows screen looks very different from the empty DOS command screen. At first, it may seem that learning to use Windows (with its icons, menus, scroll bars, and other tools) is more difficult than learning to use DOS, but this is not the case. Learning to use Windows is not very difficult. It does, however, require you to learn how Windows accesses programs, what type of program is written for Windows, and how to use the various Windows controls. This is the goal of this chapter.

The reason a chapter on Windows is included in a book on ClarisWorks is simple—ClarisWorks for Windows requires Microsoft Windows to operate. Windows is a completely different environment from DOS. It is so different that many software manufacturers design programs specifically to operate under Windows. ClarisWorks for Windows is just such a program. ClarisWorks for Windows will not work without Microsoft Windows operating and controlling the computer. Therefore, if you do not have Microsoft Windows, you cannot use ClarisWorks.

Finally, this chapter will not make you a Microsoft Windows expert. Instead, this chapter is designed to get you started. There is a lot to learning all the intricacies of Microsoft Windows. As you become more and more skilled, you will likely pick up many Windows features. For now, concern yourself with the basics discussed in this chapter. You can become a Windows expert another time.

STARTING WINDOWS

In most cases, starting Windows is as simple as turning on your computer. Most people install Windows to execute every time they turn on the computer. There are some important issues related to installing Windows, but these are fully discussed in the installation procedures section of the Windows manual.

Assuming Windows resides on your computer and is set to launch each time you turn on your computer, the first thing to do is start your computer. If you do not get a screen that looks similar to Figure 1-1, then Windows is probably not installed or is not installed to execute when the computer is turned on. If this is the case, check with your instructor or follow the installation procedures provided with the Windows manual.

THE MOUSE

The one piece of hardware most closely associated with Windows is the mouse. While a mouse is not required to operate Windows, almost everyone who uses Windows uses a mouse. The reason is simple—mouse controls are available for virtually all Windows activities. Therefore, it is a good idea to learn to use a mouse before you attempt too many other tasks. Fortunately, learning to use a mouse is very simple.

On virtually every screen in Windows there is an arrow (or some other symbol) known as the *mouse pointer* or simply, *pointer*. Moving the mouse across a flat surface moves the pointer on the screen. To issue a command or start a program, move the pointer onto the desired selection, then press the left mouse button two times in rapid succession. This is known as *double clicking*. Sometimes you need to click the mouse button only one time. This process is known as *point and click*.

Developing the requisite hand-eye coordination with the mouse may take a bit of practice, but that is all there is to controlling the computer with a mouse.

 *Hands-On*

1. Turn on your computer.

   Make sure you check with your instructor for any start-up requirements specific to the model of computer you are using. You should see an opening screen similar to Figure 1-1.

FIGURE 1-1

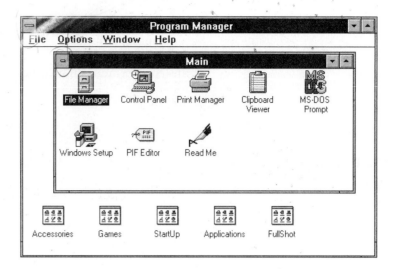

This screen may differ from yours depending on how your computer and Windows are set up.

2. Move the mouse.

   Notice that as the mouse moves on the mouse pad, so does the small arrow (pointer) onscreen.

3. Move the pointer until it points to the word *Help* in the upper portion of the screen.

4. Click and hold down on the mouse button.

   This produces a list of Help menu options, as in Figure 1-2.

5. Move the mouse pointer down the screen without releasing the mouse button. This is called *dragging*. Drag the mouse down until About Program Manager is highlighted.

6. Release the mouse button.

   This will activate a message telling which version of Windows you are using, as well as information about your computer and the product license. The figures in this chapter are from Microsoft Windows 3.1; if you have another version, some of the procedures may differ slightly. See Figure 1-3.

7. The About Microsoft Windows message is contained within a *window* (hence the software's name). Move the pointer onto the small box in the upper left corner of this message screen or window. This box is called the *Control Menu*. Click the mouse button, drag to highlight Close, then release the mouse button.

   Notice that selecting Close closes this box.

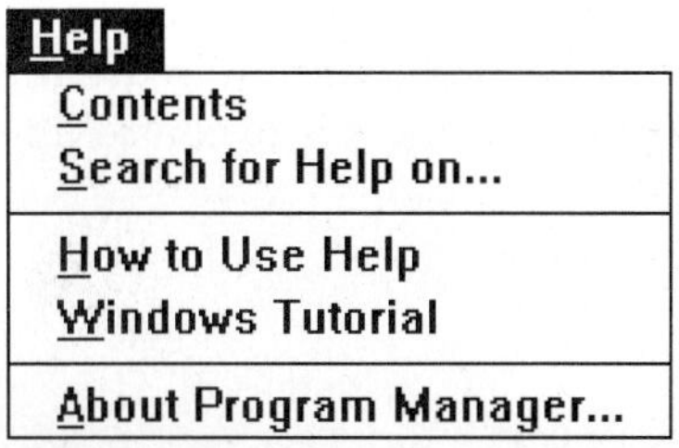

Help

Contents
Search for Help on...

How to Use Help
Windows Tutorial

About Program Manager...

FIGURE 1-2

FIGURE 1-3

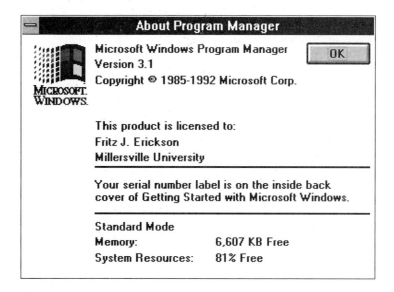

WINDOWS

When you start Windows, a very special program goes into effect. This program is called the *Program Manager.* As with all programs within Windows, the Program Manager is found on a screen called the Windows *desktop.* The Windows desktop is like your own desktop, but instead of holding pads of paper and pencil holders, the Windows desktop holds windows.

All Windows activities occur within a window. If you want to run a program, that program runs in a window. If you want to create a word processing document, that document is created in a window. If you want to group programs together, that group is in a window. So the most important part of learning how to use Windows is learning how to control each window.

Window Components

It is not by accident that this is called Microsoft Windows—everything you do is done in a window. Fortunately, every window is made up of the same basic components. This standardization helps make learning to use and control Windows very easy. Once you learn the parts of one window, you will be able to use any window in any program. The following is a list of the common window components. Figure 1-4 shows these components.

Control Menu box Every window has a Control Menu box that, when selected, allows you access to several window controlling commands. One of these commands is Close. Selecting this option closes the window.

FIGURE 1-4

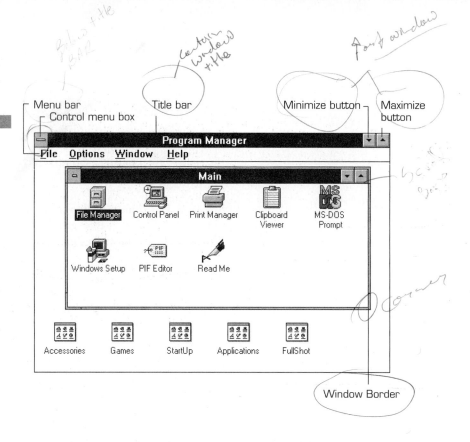

Menu bar
Control menu box
Title bar
Minimize button
Maximize button
Window Border

(handwritten annotations:) Relic title BAR · Center window title · front window · corner · Win menu's

Title bar and title The title bar appears across the top of every window. Inside the title bar is the window title. Typically, the title bar is a different color or shade when that window is active.

Minimize and maximize buttons Every window can be reduced to an icon by clicking on the minimize button. An icon is a graphic representation, or picture, of a program or a group of programs. The maximize button enlarges a window to fill the entire desktop.

Menu bar Below the title bar is the menu bar. This component contains all menus associated with the window. The contents of the menu bar differ slightly, depending on the program that is running in the window. For example, the menus in the menu bar are somewhat different for the ClarisWorks window than for the Microsoft Word window.

Scroll bars Scroll bars are often available to allow you access to different areas within a window. Often a window displays only a portion of what is available in that window. The scroll bars allow you to view all information contained within a window.

Window border Every window is surrounded by a window border. The border not only identifies the boundaries of the window, but serves as a tool for changing the size and shape of a window. By pointing at any border and clicking the mouse button, the pointer changes to a bi-directional arrow. Dragging this arrow changes the size of the window. Clicking on the corners allows you to change both the height and width of a window.

Window Types

There are three different types of windows available on the desktop — applications windows, document windows, and group windows. Applications windows contain programs running under Windows. In the next chapter, when you start to run ClarisWorks for Windows, it will run as an application in an application window. Document windows do not appear on the desktop, but rather as a window within an applications window. When you learn to use the ClarisWorks word processor, your word processing documents will be created in a document window inside of the ClarisWorks program window. Finally, there are group windows. Group windows are organizational tools that contain icons (pictures that represent other windows). A group window may contain several program icons. When you select one of these icons, a program window appears.

The Program Manager

The Program Manager is the most important window of all. This application is designed to manage all other windows. It is through the Program Manager that you actually control most of the activities within Windows. The Program Manager is really an access and organizational tool.

The Program Manager is an *access* tool because you must use the Program Manager to access application windows. When you install a program such as ClarisWorks within Windows, it resides within the Program Manager. You cannot access ClarisWorks without going through the Program Manager. Virtually all other available Windows software resides within the Program Manager. The Program Manager is also an *organizational* tool because it controls group windows. Group windows are also only available within the Program Manager.

Most operations accomplished through Windows begin and end with the Program Manager. In fact, windows that are open in the Program Manager stay open only within the Program Manager and cannot be placed directly on the desktop. For all practical purposes, it is the Program Manager that you use to control Windows.

UNDERSTANDING AND SELECTING ICONS

When you start Windows, the two features that stand out most are windows and icons. Windows and icons are closely related. In fact, an icon is nothing more than a small picture representing a window. Double clicking on an icon opens a window. When you close a window, it becomes an icon.

Handwritten notes in margin:
PROGRAM ICON
GROUP ICON
Dll program Icon

There is one notable exception to the relationship of windows and icons—icons that represent programs not written to work with Windows do not open a window. Instead, these icons automatically launch the program as if you were directly in DOS and outside of Windows. The reason is simple. Not all programs written to run on an IBM or IBM compatible computer were designed to work directly with Windows; nevertheless, many Windows users still like to use these programs. Windows accommodates these programs by allowing icons to represent non-Windows programs (usually called DOS programs). When you finish using a DOS program, Windows returns and the program returns as an icon.

Icon Types

There are two types of icons in Windows. The first type is the program icon. These represent programs that run either directly under Windows or DOS. Double clicking on any program icon launches the program. The second type is the group icon. Group icons represent windows, the sole purpose of which is to organize program icons. Double clicking on a group icon opens a group window. Inside the group window are program icons. For example, you may have a group icon called Communications. Double clicking on this icon will produce a window with all your communications software program icons. If you have more than one word processor, you might choose to have a group called Word Processing. By organizing programs in group windows, you can keep related programs together.

PUTTING WINDOWS AND ICONS TO WORK

One powerful feature of Windows is its ability to display more than one window at a time. For example, clicking on an applications icon in the Program Manager launches that application as a window (assuming it is a Windows application). You can return to the Program Manager without exiting the program, then click on a second icon to open a second application. Both applications can run together, either on the desktop or within the Program Manager.

Though several windows may be open at any one time, only one window may be active. To activate an open window, move the pointer anywhere in the window and click the mouse button. On a color monitor, the title bar of the active window is a different color than all other windows on the desktop.

There can be one problem with multiple windows open, especially within the Program Manager. Since windows can share the same space, it is possible that one window will sit wholly on top of another. In other words, one window will be hidden by another. If this happens, you need to adjust the size of the top window, or move the top window, to make the other window accessible.

Drag title bar

Moving Windows

The window title bar is very useful. It not only contains the name of the window, but also serves as a tool for moving windows. By clicking, holding, and dragging the title bar you can move a window to any location you want. The color of the title bar also shows whether the window is active.

Adjusting Windows

With group windows, it is common for only some of the icons contained within the window to appear. With document windows, there may be much more than appears in the window. (By analogy, when you look into a room through a window, you see only part of the room.) There are three primary ways to see additional information. First, you can expand the size of the window by clicking and dragging any of the window borders. Second, you can click on the maximize button. This causes the window to expand to fill the desktop. Finally, you can use the scroll bars to move the contents within the window. Arrows at either end of the scroll bar move icons or your application's data in the window up, down, left, or right.

Scroll bars are available only when there is more information within the window than appears on screen. For example, with group windows, the scroll bars only appear when there are more icons present than can appear in the window. This occurs when there are too many icons to display in the window, or the window is too small to display all the icons. If all icons appear within the window, the scroll bars do not. If there are no icons below the window but there are some to the left or right, only the horizontal scroll bars appear.

Moving Icons

Not only can you move windows to new locations within the Program Manager or desktop, you can also move icons within a window. Clicking, holding, and dragging an icon is all there is to moving an icon. In the Program Manager, you can also drag icons from one window to another. This allows you to create new group windows, then move related icons from any other window to a newly-created group window.

 *Hands-On*

1. In most cases, starting Microsoft Windows automatically launches the Program Manager. Click on the maximize arrow in the upper right corner.

   The Program Manager window expands to fill the entire desktop—Figure 1-5. If the Program Manager window is already expanded, clicking on this button reduces its size.

FIGURE 1-5

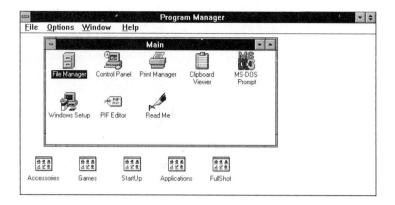

2. Assuming ClarisWorks for Windows resides in the Claris-Works group, double click on this icon.

    This opens another window containing all the ClarisWorks for Windows icons (ClarisWorks and Read Me). See Figure 1-6.

3. Locate the Accessories group icon and double-click.

    This opens the Accessories window, pictured in Figure 1-7.

4. Using the window borders, adjust the size of each open window so that no windows overlap.

5. Click and hold on the Read Me icon in the ClarisWorks window.

6. Drag this icon into the Accessories window and release the mouse button.

    Notice that the icon moves from one window to another, as shown in Figure 1-8.

FIGURE 1-6

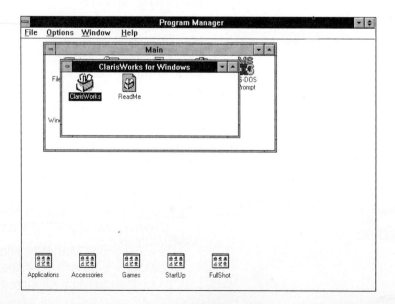

FIGURE 1-7

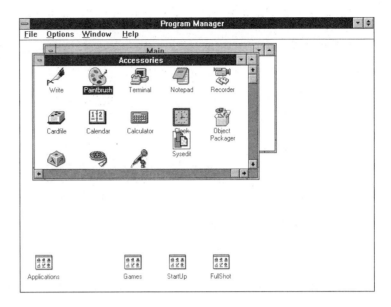

7. Move the Read Me icon back to the ClarisWorks window.

8. Activate the ClarisWorks window, then click on the Control Menu box and select the Close option.

   This closes this window and the ClarisWorks icon appears.

9. Click and hold on the title bar of the Accessories window and drag this window to a new location within the Program Manager.

   Clicking on and dragging the title bar moves the entire window.

FIGURE 1-8

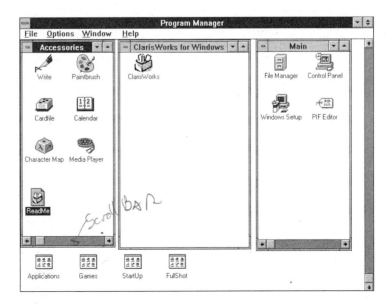

10. Adjust the size of the Accessories window so that only one icon in the window is visible.

11. Practice using the scroll bars and scroll arrows to view different portions of the window.

12. Return the Accessories window to a size at which all icons in the window are visible.

13. Open the ClarisWorks window.

14. Double click on the ClarisWorks icon.

    Instead of opening another window, double clicking on a program icon launches the program. The opening screen is shown in Figure 1-9.

15. We are not quite ready to start working in ClarisWorks, so exit the program and return to the Program Manager. To do this, move the mouse and click once on Cancel. Next, click and hold the mouse button down on the word File. Notice that a series of menu options appears. Keeping the mouse button depressed, drag and select Exit, then release the mouse button. See Figure 1-10.

FIGURE 1-9

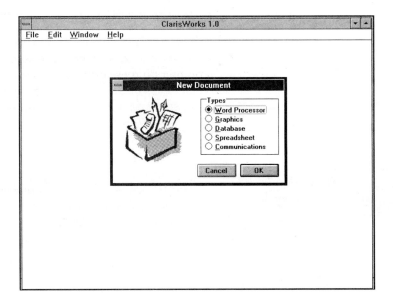

USING MENUS

Windows provides several menus and menu options for additional control. While it is beyond the scope of this chapter to discuss every option, a few options are especially important.

File	Edit	Window	Help
New...		Ctrl+N	
Open...		Ctrl+O	
Insert...			
Close		Ctrl+W	
Save		Ctrl+S	
Save As...		Shift+Ctrl+S	
Macros			▶
Mail Merge...		Shift+Ctrl+M	
Print Setup...			
Print...		Ctrl+P	
Exit		Ctrl+Q	

FIGURE 1-10

The common term for a menu in Windows is *pull-down menu.* Pull-down menus provide several important options for almost every program. In fact, the pull-down menu option in Windows is much the same for all programs—word processors, databases, spreadsheets, and all other software packages that run under Windows. This is one reason why programs controlled by Windows are easy to learn and use. After learning to use pull-down menus for one program, many of the commands are the same for every other program. For example, selecting Save is much the same for all Windows-based programs.

Across the top of the Program Manager window is a list of available pull-down menus. These are the File, Options, Window, and Help menus. In addition, to the left of the title bar is the Control Menu box. The Control Menu box contains several options, including Restore, Move, Size, Minimize, Maximize, Close, and Switch To. These options allow you to control much of a window. For example, selecting Minimize from the Control Menu box is the same as clicking on the Minimize button.

Selecting a menu option begins by activating the pull-down menu. All you need do is place the pointer on the desired menu name and click the mouse button. A list of all available options appears. Darker items are available for selection. Lighter, or shadowed, options are not currently available and cannot be selected. To select an available option, move the pointer onto the desired option and click the mouse button. You may also click and hold on a menu title and drag the mouse to highlight a desired option. With this method, releasing the mouse button executes the highlighted menu option.

Some options produce secondary menus. That is, placing the pointer on these options causes another menu to appear. Select items from a secondary pull-down menu by dragging the pointer down the secondary menu onto the desired option, then releasing the mouse button.

 *Hands-On*

1. Time to explore! The menus in the Program Manager provide a variety of controlling features. Don't be afraid to select any option you want. If you get to a window and don't know what to do, try selecting Cancel.

2. Be sure to try all of the options in the Window menu. Notice especially the effects of the Cascade, Tile, and Arrange Icons options.

USING DIALOG BOXES

Another useful Windows feature is that most applications use the same basic design for accessing data and controlling menus. There may be some variation from program to program, but most are similar. Most programs have the Save, Save As, and Open options.

Another standard feature is the use of special screens or windows to help make decisions about controlling the software. These special screens or windows are known as *dialog boxes* because they are the point at which users converse directly with the software. As with other features, the design and use of dialog boxes is standard from program to program.

A very important dialog box handles the saving and retrieving of files from disks. For example, after launching a word processing program and creating a new document, it is important to save the document to a disk. Selecting Save As from the File menu produces the Save As dialog box.

Dialog boxes that manage the saving and retrieving of files always have three important features—drives, directories, and file name. First, every time you save a file, you must specify the *drive* location of the file. This is accomplished by selecting the desired drive letter. In most of the examples in this text, the desired drive will be A:. This is almost always the first floppy disk of your computer. Second, *directories* allows you to specify a directory from the group of directories found on a disk. Most users do not have multiple directories for their floppy disk; however, there are almost always multiple directories for the hard drive. If you are saving on the hard drive you must specify the desired directory. Finally, the *File Name* box. In this box, you specify the exact name of the file. You are limited to eight characters plus a three-character extension. For now, don't use the extension. ClarisWorks will provide the necessary extension.

Loading or retrieving a file produces a very similar dialog box. Again, you must specify three factors— drives, directories, and file name. Below the File Name box is a list of all available files from the selected drive and directory. If one of these is the desired file, all you need do is click once on the file name, then click on OK.

Dialog boxes almost always have two buttons— OK and Cancel. Cancel is available in most dialog boxes as a means of leaving the dialog box without invoking any of the available selections. If you accidentally select a menu that produces a dialog box, use the Cancel button. Clicking on OK accepts and executes all settings within the dialog box. It is not enough to click on an item or insert information into a dialog box, you must click on OK to complete the process. In many cases, double clicking on a dialog box selection has the same effect as clicking once on the selection then clicking on OK. This is provided as a shortcut, and the decision is up to you— double click or click then click again on OK.

Hands-On

1. Dialog boxes are in programs that run under Windows, so the only way to practice using dialog boxes is to use a program such as ClarisWorks. All of the processes for using and controlling dialog boxes are presented in detail throughout the rest of this text.

HELP AND THE WINDOWS TUTORIAL

Some of the most useful Windows features appear as options in the Help menu. Help allows you to obtain information onscreen about Windows. Help is so popular that many programs have the same basic Help process.

When you select the Help menu from the Program Manager, five options appear— Contents, Search for Help on.., How to Use Help, Windows Tutorial, and About Program Manager. Contents and Search for Help on.. allow you to locate specific Help topics. When you select Contents, a table of Help contents appears. You can select any topic from the contents to receive further instruction. If you are not sure which area within the contents is appropriate for your problem or concern, Search for Help on.. is always available. With this option, you can type a topic name and Windows will help you locate information within the help feature about the topic.

The easiest way to learn to use Help is through the How to Use Help option in the Help menu. This option takes you step-by-step through the Help process.

Another very useful feature of the Help menu is the Windows Tutorial. Selecting this option produces an on-line tutorial to guide you through the basic steps of using Windows. If you are having any trouble controlling your computer through Windows, use the Windows Tutorial option. This will provide you with direct instruction.

Hands-On

1. From the Program Manager window, select the Help menu.

   Notice that this menu contains five options, shown in Figure 1-11.

2. Select the Contents option from the Help menu.

   This produces a window containing Contents of Program Manager Help. See Figure 1-12.

3. Within the Help window, select Window Menu Commands.

   This produces an explanation of all options within the Window menu. See Figure 1-13.

4. Click on the Search button.

   The Search dialog box appears.

5. Type **icons**.

   Notice that the list of topics changes.

Help
<u>C</u>ontents
<u>S</u>earch for Help on...
<u>H</u>ow to Use Help
<u>W</u>indows Tutorial
<u>A</u>bout Program Manager...

FIGURE 1-11

FIGURE 1-12

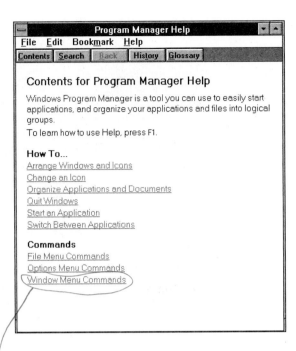

6. Click on the Go To button.

   An explanation of icons appears in the Help window.

7. Select Exit from the File menu of the Program Manager Help window. This closes the Help feature.

FIGURE 1-13

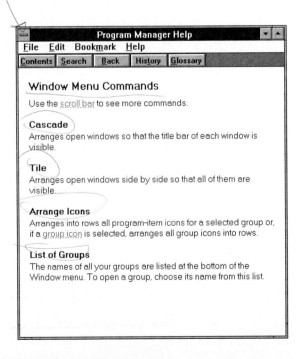

Summary

- The operating system popular on IBM and IBM compatible computers is DOS (MS-DOS and PC-DOS).

- DOS is a command-driven operating system.

- Microsoft Windows is a graphical user interface (GUI) that automates many of the controlling features of DOS.

- The hardware that is linked to Windows is a mouse.

- The Program Manager helps you organize information on the desktop.

- Every window contains a Control Menu Box, title bar and title, minimize and maximize buttons, menu bar, scroll bars, and a window border.

- There are three different types of windows on the desktop—applications windows, document windows, and group windows.

- Double clicking on an icon opens a window.

- Program icons represent programs that run either directly under Windows or are DOS-based programs.

- Group icons represent group windows, the sole purpose of which is to organize program icons.

- Though several windows may be open at any one time, only one window may be active.

- Dialog boxes allow users to communicate with Windows.

- Dialog boxes that manage the saving and retrieving of files always have three important features—drive, directory, and file name.

- Help allows you to obtain information about Windows onscreen.

- Through Help, you can access an on-line tutorial to guide you through the basic steps of using Windows.

Questions

1. The operating system most popular for IBM and IBM compatible computers is known as _DOS_ .

2. The _Title bar_ appears at the top of every window and contains the name of the window.

3. Scroll bars are available only if _other information icons_ are present in the window but do not appear on the screen.

4. Windows makes using a _____personal_____ computer much easier and more efficient.

5. Clicking a mouse button twice in rapid succession is known as _____Double clicking_____ .

6. In Windows, the desktop holds _____Windows_____ .

7. The _____Title bar_____ appears across the top of each window.

8. An _____Icon_____ is a graphic representation, or picture, of a program or a group of programs.

9. _____Menu's_____ are often available to allow you access to different areas within a window.

10. There are three different types of windows available: desktop—_____Application_____ windows, _____Document_____ windows, and _____Group_____ windows.

Quiz

1. The set of commands that controls IBM and IBM compatible computers is called
   a. System
   b. OS
   c. DOS
   d. MC-DOS

2. Most users control Windows via
   a. the mouse
   b. the keyboard
   c. the mousekey
   d. the keymouse

3. *Dragging* the mouse means to:
   a. click the mouse two times in rapid succession
   b. hold down the mouse button and move the mouse
   c. click twice on two different commands
   d. move the mouse on the palm of your hand

4. Windows replaces DOS. *operating system Dos.*
   a. true
   b. false

5. The desktop:
   a. is the location on which the computer resides
   b. is really a disk
   c. is a screen location
   d. resides within a window

6. The common term for the menus across the top is:
   a. desktop menus
   b. menus
   c. pull-down menus
   d. Locator

7. Which icon represents text created with a word processor?
   a. program icon
   b. document icon
   c. group icon
   d. disk icon

organizes other program icons

8. Which type of icon most commonly contains other icons?
   a. program icon   b. document icon
   c. group icon   d. disk icon

9. Once a window is open, it may *not* be moved to a new location on the desktop.
   a. true   b. false

10. The primary control program within Windows is the:
    a. Control Program   b. Program Manager
    c. Control Manager   d. Program Control

Applications

1. Use the Windows Tutorial option found in the Help menu of the Program Manager. This option will take you on a guided tutorial of the basic procedures of using Windows. Even if you have some experience with Windows, you will be surprised how much you can learn about this software.

2. For those new to computers, learning to use the mouse takes a bit of hand-eye coordination practice. Practice moving the mouse to select different icons and drag windows. The more comfortable you become with the mouse now, the easier it will be later to use the mouse to control ClarisWorks for Windows.

3. Select How to Use Help. This option in the Help menu provides you with a good overview of locating specific Help topics. It is a good idea to know Help now, before you really need help.

CLARISWORKS ESSENTIALS

OBJECTIVES

Learning the material in this chapter will enable you to:

- describe why ClarisWorks for Windows is integrated software
- identify the five ClarisWorks document types
- identify the advantages of using an integrated software package
- format a new floppy disk
- correctly start ClarisWorks
- identify the major components of the ClarisWorks environment
- create, save, and print a word processing document
- correctly exit ClarisWorks

WHAT IS CLARISWORKS FOR WINDOWS?

For many computer users, ClarisWorks is all the software they will ever need. The reason is simple—ClarisWorks for Windows is *integrated* computer software. That is, ClarisWorks is several different types of software in one convenient, easy-to-use package. ClarisWorks is a word processor, a spreadsheet, a database, a telecommunications program, and a graphics program.

For many people who use computers, the five types of software available in ClarisWorks are sufficient for their computer activities. The most popular type of computer software is word processing. Word processing software makes it easy and efficient to create, edit, and print text. The word processing component of ClarisWorks provides the tools needed to create a variety of high-quality documents. Having a means for efficiently entering and editing text makes ClarisWorks indispensable to users.

Spreadsheet software is a tool for performing numeric calculations. Just as a word processor provides the tools for effectively manipulating text, a spreadsheet provides the tools for effectively manipulating numbers. The spreadsheet found within ClarisWorks is a powerful, yet easy-to-use tool for designing budgets, calculating student grades, generating financial forecasts, developing loan

20

information, completing tax records, generating statistical analyses, and a host of other activities.

Database software makes it possible to store and recall large amounts of information quickly and easily. For example, student databases are common in schools and universities for maintaining information on students. With database software, it is possible to quickly locate a student's transcripts, produce class schedules, do graduation audits, maintain address lists, create telephone directories, and a number of other applications for which maintaining information in an organized fashion is crucial. The ClarisWorks database makes it possible to not only store and retrieve large sets of data, but produce reports that are as attractive as those produced by a word processor.

Producing images is the goal of graphics programs. With the drawing features found in ClarisWorks' graphics program, it is possible for computer users to create pictures, develop illustrations, produce logos, and modify predesigned images.

The communications portion of ClarisWorks is the tool that makes it possible for your computer to communicate with other computers. Communications allow one computer to send and receive information to and from other computers. By using the communications features within ClarisWorks, users can access databases, send electronic mail, send and receive files to any other computer, share programs, do electronic shopping and banking, and even play chess with other computer chess enthusiasts anywhere in the world.

All these features in one simple, easy-to-use package provides computer users with almost all of the software that they will ever need. In addition to providing a great deal of software in one package, there are several distinct advantages to using an integrated package such as ClarisWorks. First is the commonality of controls from one application to another. Once you learn how to use one part of ClarisWorks, the same basic structure applies to each of the other components. In other words, the way you interact with the software stays constant within ClarisWorks. If you were to purchase separate word processing, spreadsheet, and database software, you would have to learn the usage and terminology differences for each software package. ClarisWorks standardizes the language and terminology and provides a similar interface. For example, saving a file with the word processing component is done the same as saving a file with the spreadsheet component.

In addition to consistency, another advantage of ClarisWorks is its ability to transfer files from one application to another. For example, taking information created on a spreadsheet and moving it into a word processor is a snap with ClarisWorks. If you were to use two separate programs from different software publishers, transferring data might not be so easy.

ClarisWorks is also ideal for learning the basic concepts of the major applications. Even if you plan to use a different word processor, spreadsheet, or database, learning the concepts of each of these in one environment makes it easier to learn to use separate packages. In other words, once you learn to use the word processor in Claris-Works, you will find it very easy to learn and use almost any other brand of word processing software.

While there are advantages to using an integrated package, there is one potential disadvantage. Because ClarisWorks does so many things, it does not have all of the features found in some single-purpose software. For example, while the word processing qualities of ClarisWorks are extensive, there are some capabilities not included that are available in other software packages. Typically these are the more advanced features, which only a very small number of people might use. A simple example is indexing. The word processing portion of ClarisWorks does not provide a means of generating an automatic index. However, unless you plan to write, typeset, and publish a book, this will not be a major concern.

BEFORE YOU BEGIN

Before you begin to learn each of the major components of Claris-Works, there are a few things to be addressed. The first has to do with storing the documents you generate with ClarisWorks. All components in ClarisWorks allow you to create and store documents on a disk. In fact, the term *document* is used with each component. You will create word processing documents, spreadsheet documents, database documents, and so forth. One concern is where you will keep all these documents. The answer is on your own floppy disk.

Formatting Disks

Before you begin, you must have a disk prepared for storing your documents. While it is possible to save documents on the hard disk of your computer, there are a number of problems with this approach. If you store documents on one computer, you may use only that computer. Also, if you are working in a lab setting, saving documents on a hard disk makes them accessible to others. Unless you are using ClarisWorks on a network *and* you have a security code, save your documents on your own floppy disk. However, before saving a document to a new disk, you must first prepare that disk. This preparation is known as *formatting*.

Formatting a disk in Windows is very easy. First, launch Windows—usually, this means just starting your computer. In the Main group is a program called the File Manager. This program provides direct control over all files on all disks. It also contains the process for formatting disks. Therefore, just open the Main window and double click on the File Manager icon.

In the menu bar of the File Manager is the Disk menu. In this menu is the Format Disk option. Selecting Format from the Disk menu begins the process of formatting your disk. When you select Format Disk, a dialog box appears. In this Format Disk dialog box you must provide two important pieces of information. First, you must identify the location of the disk you want to format. In most cases Disk In: should be set to Drive A: (this is the first floppy disk drive). However, this can be changed to any other drive. Second, you must specify the capacity. The capacity of your disk is determined by two factors—the capability of your floppy disk drive and the type of disk you insert. You must select the capacity that fits both.

The options in Capacity: are set according to the capacity of your disk drive. In most cases, there are two options. If your disk is labeled HD (for High Density), select the higher capacity. If your disk is labeled DD (for Double Density), select the lower capacity. If only one capacity selection is available, you must use a DD or double-density disk.

Once you have specified the Disk In: and Capacity:, the next step is to insert the disk you want to format and click on OK. You may get a message reminding you that formatting will erase all data on the disk. If this is a new disk, then click on Yes. However, if this is a previously formatted disk, you must be sure that it is okay to lose all information. Once a disk is formatted, any existing information on it is lost. If you are not completely sure, click on No and get another disk.

Once you click on Yes to confirm formatting, another dialog box appears indicating that the disk is now being formatted. Once the format is complete, you can format another disk or click on No to return to the File Manager. From the File Manager, select Exit from the File Menu to return to the Program Manager.

Hands-On

1. Turn on your computer.

    Assuming Microsoft Windows is correctly installed and set to launch at start up, in a moment or two you should see the Program Manager shown in Figure 2-1.

2. Check to see if the Main window is open. If not, locate the Main group icon and double click on it. See Figure 2-1.

    Locate the File Manager icon.

3. Double click on the File Manager icon.

    This launches the File Manager. Notice that a special window containing a list of files appears.

4. From the Disk menu, select Format Disk.

    This produces the Format Disk dialog box shown in Figure 2-2.

5. Assuming that you want to format a disk in the A drive, make sure Drive A: appears next to Disk In:. See Figure 2-2.

    If not, or if you want to select Drive B:, click on Drive A: then select Drive B:.

FIGURE 2-1

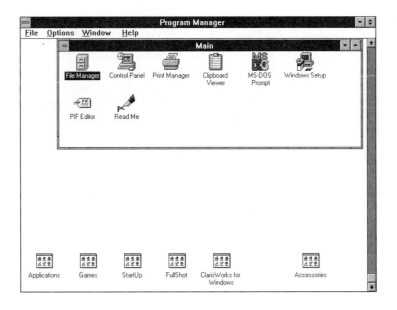

6. Next to Capacity:, select the appropriate disk density.

   Look at the disk you want to format. If it is DD, or double-density, select the lower capacity. If your disk has an HD, select the higher. Put your disk in the drive.

7. Make sure the disk you want to format is in the correct drive and click on OK.

   Notice the Confirm Format Disk dialog box, shown in Figure 2-3.

8. Click on Yes (or No if you want to format a different disk) and watch the Formatting Disk dialog box.

9. If you do not want to format another disk, click on No when asked if you want to format another.

10. Using the File menu in the menu bar, select Exit.

    This will close and leave the File Manager and return you to the Program Manager.

FIGURE 2-2

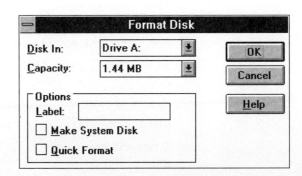

FIGURE 2-3

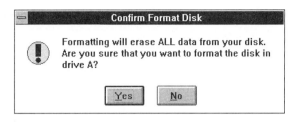

Confirm Format Disk

Formatting will erase ALL data from your disk. Are you sure that you want to format the disk in drive A?

Yes   No

11. Take out the disk you just formatted, write your name on it and the label ClarisWorks Learn Disk. This disk will be used throughout the rest of this book.

Be sure to use a felt-tip pen for writing on disks. Ballpoint pens can harm disks.

STARTING CLARISWORKS FOR WINDOWS

Now that you have a formatted disk, it's time to start ClarisWorks for Windows. As discussed in Chapter 1, launching any application is done by opening the group window containing the desired program icon, then double clicking on that icon. Assuming ClarisWorks resides in the ClarisWorks group window, open the ClarisWorks group window and double click on the ClarisWorks program icon.

If you are using a computer connected to a network, the process for locating and launching ClarisWorks may be slightly different. Please consult your instructor or lab technician for the correct procedures.

After double clicking on the ClarisWorks icon, in a few moments ClarisWorks displays a New Document dialog box. Since ClarisWorks is actually five programs in one, the very first decision to make is which of the five types of documents you wish to create. While it is possible to work on more than one document (and document type) at the same time, you must start by identifying the first document. Identify the first document by clicking on the document type, then clicking on the OK button. If you do not wish to create a new document and would rather work on an existing document, click on the Cancel button.

Hands-On

1. Open the ClarisWorks group window.

2. Inside this window is the ClarisWorks program icon. Double click on this icon.

You have successfully launched ClarisWorks if a dialog box for a new document appears, as shown in Figure 2-4.

FIGURE 2-4

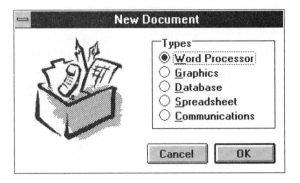

3. Since you have not yet created a document in Claris-Works, you must use this dialog box to select the type of document to create. Click once on Spreadsheet and notice that the button next to Spreadsheet becomes active.

4. Click once on Word Processing to select the ClarisWorks word processor, then click on OK.

   The word processing component of ClarisWorks is activated. See Figure 2-5.

5. Select the Exit option in the File menu.

   Since you did not modify this document, selecting Exit quits the word processing document and terminates Claris-Works.

FIGURE 2-5

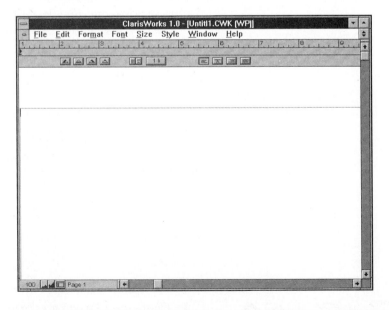

Exercise 2-1 Take a few minutes to practice starting ClarisWorks with each of the five types of documents listed in the New Document dialog box. Be sure to notice how each document window differs among the five major ClarisWorks components.

CLARISWORKS' ENVIRONMENT

Half the battle of learning to use any new piece of software is learning the software's operating environment. Two advantages make learning the operating environment of ClarisWorks efficient. First, ClarisWorks uses the same look and feel as virtually all other Windows software—once you have learned how to use Windows, learning to use ClarisWorks becomes much easier. Second, the same basic process used to create a word processing document is used for each of the other five types of documents. Therefore, we have selected the ClarisWorks word processor to describe the basic operating environment. From this discussion, it should be easy to learn the environment of each of the other document types.

With all Microsoft Windows software, the primary controlling feature is the menu bar. This is located below the title bar and is filled with menu names such as File, Edit, Format, Font, Size, Style, Window, and Help. The items in the ClarisWorks menu bar change to suit the document type. For example, the menu bar for the communications component is different from the word processing menu bar. In either case, menus provide the same basic vehicle for controlling the software.

Another controlling feature of ClarisWorks is the tool panel. This is located along the left side of the screen. The panel's tools each represent some aspect of ClarisWorks. For example, there is a tool for generating text, another tool for drawing a line, even a tool for coloring circles. As with menus in the menu bar, the tools within the tool panel change depending on document type. Figure 2-6 identifies the tools for a word processing document.

Every document generated in ClarisWorks is created within a document window. Document windows work and are controlled in

FIGURE 2-6

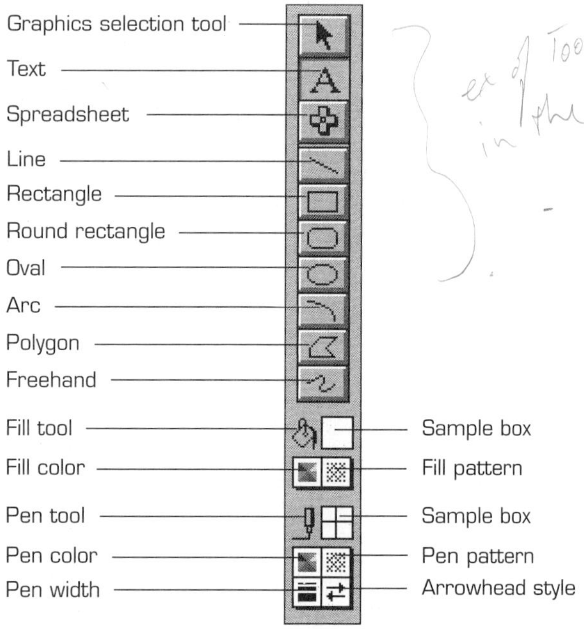

Graphics selection tool
Text
Spreadsheet
Line
Rectangle
Round rectangle
Oval
Arc
Polygon
Freehand
Fill tool — Sample box
Fill color — Fill pattern
Pen tool — Sample box
Pen color — Pen pattern
Pen width — Arrowhead style

the same way as any other window. Each document window has a title bar, Control Menu box, minimize button, maximize button, and, when needed, scroll bars. There are, of course, some differences. The title bar of a document window within ClarisWorks identifies the name and type of document. The document type appears in parentheses next to the document name.

Closing a document window allows you to exit a document without exiting ClarisWorks. If you have not added or changed information in the document window and select Close from the Control Menu box, ClarisWorks will not ask you whether to save the document. However, if you have made changes or additions, Claris-Works will prompt you to save the document. At this point, do not save your documents.

Any time ClarisWorks is without a document window, the menu bar offers only a few options. One is the New option in the File menu. Selecting New produces the same New Document dialog box found when first starting ClarisWorks. This option is available for you to create a new document as you wish while operating ClarisWorks.

Hands-On

1. Start ClarisWorks and open a new word processing document.

2. Across the top of the screen is the menu bar containing menu items for the word processing feature of Claris-Works. Click on each of the menu items to view the contents of each pull-down menu.

3. Using the Window menu, select Show Tools.

   This causes the tool panel to appear along the left edge of the screen, as in Figure 2-7.

FIGURE 2-7

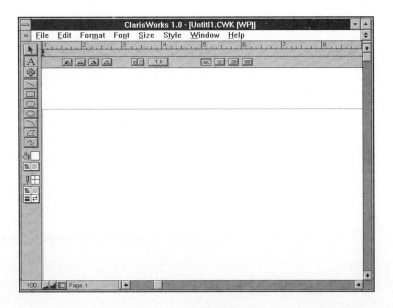

4. Make sure the ruler across the top of the word processing document window appears by selecting Show Ruler from the Window menu if necessary.

5. Notice that the document window name in the title bar contains (*WP*) marking this as a word processing document.

6. Select Close from the File menu to close the Untitl1.CWK (WP) document. Because no information was placed within the document, there is no need to save this document on disk.

   Notice that the menu bar for ClarisWorks changes significantly. See Figure 2-8.

7. Select New from the File menu.

   This produces the same New Document dialog box that first appeared when starting ClarisWorks.

8. Select Word Processing and click on OK.

FIGURE 2-8

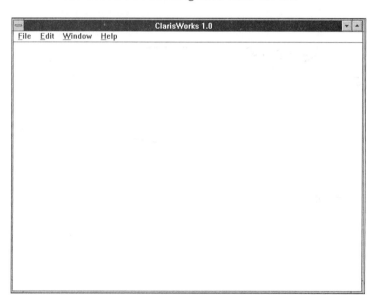

Exercise 2-2 Explore some more. Don't be afraid to spend time exploring ClarisWorks. You cannot damage anything or create problems that cannot be solved. Remember, though, if ClarisWorks asks you to save, click on Cancel. If you get to a point from which you don't know how to return, click on Cancel. (Try a warm boot if you really get lost.)

A QUICK INITIATION

A good way to get an idea of how ClarisWorks works is to create a document. Since word processing is a tool that most people use, we will take a few minutes to run through the process of creating a word processing document. The information presented here is not meant to replace the next chapter on word processing. In fact, this section will be repeated in large part in the next chapter.

When you start a document, you must first decide whether you want the tool panel to appear. For most word processing documents, the tool panel is not needed. Therefore, it is a good idea to make sure the tool panel is disabled by selecting Hide Tools from the Window menu.

(not Hide tools usually needed)

Inside the word processing document window are dotted lines. These represent the column guides. Inside the column guides is a thin, flashing line. This is the insertion point. The insertion point is the location at which text typed from the keyboard appears. In most cases, the insertion point is located at the upper left corner of the column guides.

To insert text at the insertion point, just start typing. It is possible to move the insertion point anywhere in the document, using either the mouse or the keyboard arrow keys. However, the insertion point can only be placed where text exists. In other words, you cannot move the insertion point down unless there is text there. Pressing the Return key allows you to move the cursor down and to the left one line.

The insertion point identifies the location for inserting and deleting text. Therefore, when entering or deleting text, the first step is to always put the insertion point at the desired location. This sounds simple, but it is common— even for experienced users—to forget to move the insertion point before entering or deleting text.

Delete text by pressing the Backspace key or the Del (Delete) key. Backspace always deletes one character to the left. Put the cursor one space beyond what you want to delete and press the Backspace key. The Del, or Delete, key deletes one character to the right.

Cursor. One space beyond what you want to delete w/ Backspace.
Del deletes one character to the right.

One of the exciting features of ClarisWorks is the ability to alter the appearance of text within a document. To do this, first select text, then assign an attribute to the text. Selecting text requires the use of a mouse. To select text, move the mouse pointer to the beginning of the desired text. This causes the pointer to change to an I-beam. Once the I-beam is at the beginning of what you want to select, click and hold down the left mouse button, and drag the pointer to the end of the desired text. As you drag the mouse, the text darkens (becomes *highlighted*). Releasing the mouse button completes the process of selecting text. If you make a mistake, simply try again.

Highlight (click, hold, Drag)
Selected text

After selecting text, it is easy to change its attributes by choosing among several different options. The Font, Size, and Style menus provide a list of attribute selections. Many of these will be covered in the next chapter. After choosing the desired attribute, the last step is to click the mouse to turn off the highlight.

After creating a document, there are two further steps—saving and printing. Saving any document in ClarisWorks is done by using the Save option in the File menu (Save as will be discussed later). When you save a document for the first time, the Save dialog box appears. This dialog box requires two critical pieces of information. First, you must specify the location where the file will reside. Second, you must give the file a name.

Save = Filename + Directories needed

Directory → not often

+ Drive ↑ where is disk to be copied

As discussed in Chapter 1, there are three pieces of information needed to save any document. At the top of the Save dialog box is the File Name box. This refers to the name you intend to give the file. Next to the File Name box is the Directories: box. You must specify a location on the selected disk for saving your file. If you are saving to a floppy disk, it is unlikely you will need to concern yourself with selecting a directory. However, you must concern yourself with the final selection—the drive. The Drives: box determines the drive location for the file. For all examples in this book, you will be saving to your newly formatted disk inserted in drive A:. If you are using a different drive, then you must remember to use that drive designation when saving or retrieving a file. If you fail to specify A: for the selected drive, your document will save to the hard disk. Therefore, you should always specify the drive first, followed by the directory (if any), and then the file name.

Once you have selected your drive and directory, the last step is to name your file. All newly-created files are initially given the name Untitl1.CWK, or Untitl. and a sequential number if more that one untitled file is open. Click next to the Untitl1.CWK name then press the Del or Delete key to remove this name. Once deleted, simply type the name you wish to assign to the document. After typing the name, click on Save to complete the process. After saving, the document window title bar will contain the new name of your document.

With word processing or almost any other document, after saving, the next step is to print. Printing requires that you have a correctly-installed printer. Assuming that your installation is correct, you print by selecting the Print option from the File menu. This produces a dialog box indicating which printer is selected and several additional print options. For now, don't worry about the options. Selecting OK in this dialog box starts the printing process. Usually it takes a few moments to print, so be patient. If your document fails to print, make sure the printer is turned on and has paper.

Hands-On

1. Make sure ClarisWorks is up and running and you have selected word processing for your new document. If the title bar in the document window contains (WP), then you are working on a word processing document.

2. Make sure the tool bar is hidden by selecting Hide Tools from the Window menu if necessary.

3. Notice the insertion point in the upper left corner of the column guides.

4. Type your first and last name but do not press [Enter]. See Figure 2-9.

   As you type your name, each character appears at the location of the insertion point, and the insertion point moves one space to the right.

FIGURE 2-9

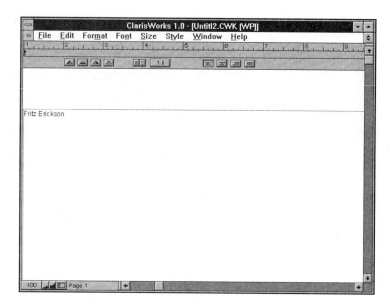

5. Press ↓.

   Notice that the insertion point does not move. This is because the insertion point can only be placed within existing text.

6. Press Enter.

   This causes the insertion point to move down one line and to the left.

7. Using the arrow keys, move the insertion point to the very beginning of your last name. Now type your middle name. See Figure 2-10.

FIGURE 2-10

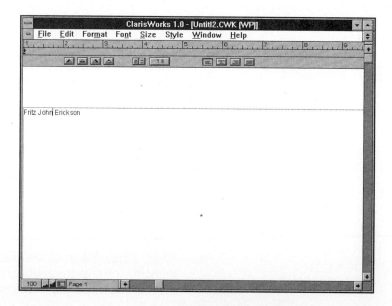

By moving the insertion point, you can insert text anywhere within a document.

8. Move the insertion point to the second line of your document and type the name of a person you like.

9. On the third line, type the name of a person you do not like.

10. Using the mouse, move the cursor to the beginning of your name. Notice that the pointer changes to an I-beam.

11. With the I-beam at the beginning of your name, click and hold the mouse button, then drag the pointer to the end of your name. With your name highlighted, release the mouse button. This selects text, as shown in Figure 2-11.

12. Select Bold under the Style menu, then click the mouse anywhere within the document.

    Your name is now in bold print.

13. Make the name of the person you do not like italic and underline the name of the person you like.

14. Now that you have created a document, it is time to save the document to your disk. Begin this process by clicking on Save in the File menu.

    This produces the Save dialog box shown in Figure 2-12.

15. You must first specify the location where the file will reside. To accomplish this, click on the box below Drives. This produces a list of all drives currently available.

FIGURE 2-11

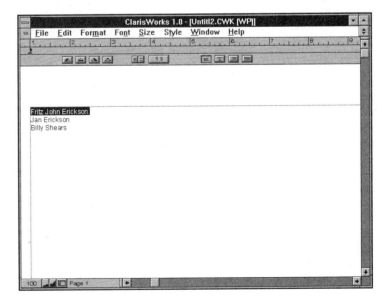

FIGURE 2-12

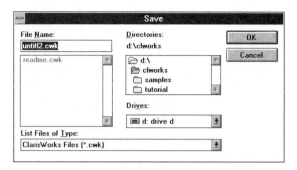

16. To select your disk, double-click on A:. (If you are using another drive, be sure to select that drive letter.)

17. Now that you have selected the location for your file, the next step is to give your file a meaningful name. Click once in the File Name box next to Untitl1.CWK then press the ⌊Del⌋ or ⌊Backspace⌋ key to delete the current name.

18. Type **NAMES.CWK**

    See Figure 2-13.

19. Click on OK. NAMES.CWK appears in the title bar, showing that you have saved your first word processing document.

20. To print your document, select the Print option from the File menu.

    This produces the Print dialog box, shown in Figure 2-14. The Print dialog box contains the name of the printer currently selected and several other options.

21. Make sure the printer is on and ready to print, then click on the OK button. In a few moments your document should appear on paper. If it doesn't, make sure the printer is on, then check with the lab assistants or your instructor for help.

    Congratulations! You have just created your first document in ClarisWorks.

FIGURE 2-13

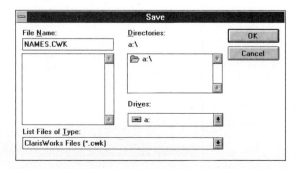

FIGURE 2-14

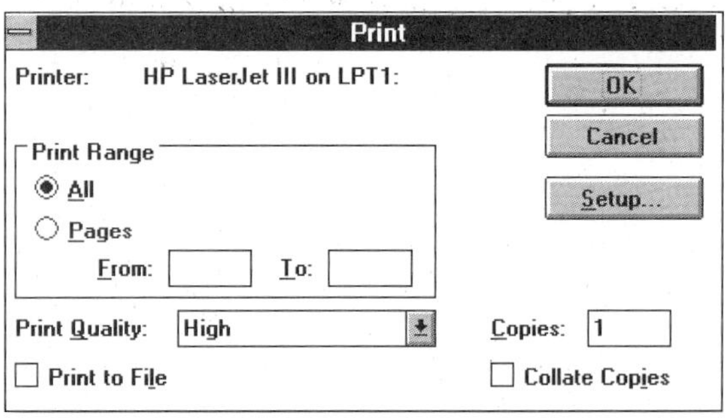

Print

Printer: HP LaserJet III on LPT1:

Print Range
- ⦿ A̲ll
- ○ P̲ages
  - F̲rom: [____]   T̲o: [____]

Print Q̲uality: [High ▼]   C̲opies: [1]

☐ Print to Fi̲le   ☐ Collate Copies

[OK]
[Cancel]
[S̲etup…]

Exercise 2-3 Now that you have created one document, try to create another. Write a letter to anyone you want. If you have not written to your mother or father, aunt, uncle, the President, or friend in a long time, this might be a good time. Be sure to save your document on your disk. Name this document LETTER1.CWK. Also, print two copies—one to send, the other to keep.

EXITING CLARISWORKS

Exiting ClarisWorks is just as important a process as creating a document. If you do it right, you will save yourself a lot of trouble later on. If you simply turn off your computer you may run into some difficulty.

To exit, select the Exit option in the File menu. If you have not saved your document, ClarisWorks will ask whether to save changes before closing. If you click on Yes, you will be given the opportunity to save your document. However, clicking on No will erase the document. Be careful. If you are not sure, *save*. Once you exit, ClarisWorks will return to the Program Manager.

 *Hands-On*

1. Select Exit from the File menu.

2. If you see the message "Save changes before closing..?" be sure to click on Yes. See Figure 2-15.

3. When you return to the Program Manager, simply turn off your computer and monitor.

FIGURE 2-15

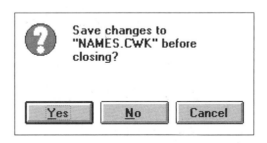

Save changes to "NAMES.CWK" before closing?

[Yes]   [No]   [Cancel]

Summary

- ClarisWorks for Windows is several different types of software wrapped into one convenient, easy-to-use package.

- ClarisWorks is a word processor, a spreadsheet, a database, a telecommunications program, and a graphics program.

- Word processing software makes it easy and efficient to create, edit, and print text.

- Spreadsheet software is a tool for performing numeric calculations.

- Database software makes it possible to store and recall large amounts of information quickly and easily.

- Graphics software makes it possible to produce images.

- Communications allows one computer to send to, and receive information from other computers.

- Preparing a disk for use is called formatting.

- The menu bar is located across the top of the screen and is filled with menu items such as File, Edit, Format, Font, Size, Style, Window, and Help.

- The menu items in the menu bar change within ClarisWorks to suit the document type.

- The tool panel is made of icons, each representing some aspect of ClarisWorks.

- Every document generated in ClarisWorks is created within a document window.

- The insertion point is the location at which all text typed from the keyboard appears.

- The Save dialog box requires the location where the file will reside and the file name.

- Exiting ClarisWorks is just as important a process as creating a document.

Questions

1. ClarisWorks for Windows is _Integrated_ computer software.

2. Because ClarisWorks for Windows does so many things, there are some _advantages_ to the features found in single purpose software.

3. Preparing a disk for a computer is called _formatting_.

4. To start ClarisWorks, simply _Double click_ on the ClarisWorks icon.

5. The _Group Window_ is made of icons, each representing some aspect of ClarisWorks.

6. The _Control Menu Box_ in the document window allows you to exit one type of document and create another.

7. It is possible to move the _Insertion_ point anywhere there is text by using either the mouse or arrow keys.

8. Deleting text is accomplished by pressing the _Delete_ key or the _Backspace_ key.

9. The two steps for saving are setting _drive_ and _File name_ .

10. If you simply _turn off_ your computer, you may run into some difficulty.

Quiz

1. Which of the following is not part of ClarisWorks for Windows?
   a. word processing
   b. desktop publishing
   c. spreadsheet
   d. communications

2. Which of the following is best for manipulating numeric information?
   a. word processor
   b. spreadsheet
   c. database
   d. graphics

3. Which of the following is not an advantage of integrated software?
   a. easier to learn
   b. more efficient to learn
   c. all components are full-featured
   d. consistent operations from one application to another

4. Which of the following prepares a disk to save files?
   a. formatting
   b. preparation
   c. erasing
   d. desktop

5. Which icon is needed to launch ClarisWorks for Windows?
   a. ClarisWorks group icon
   b. Program Manager
   c. ClarisWorks program icon
   d. all of the above

6. Which of the following appear(s) at the top of every screen?
   a. tool panel
   b. menu bar
   c. title bar
   d. all of the above

7. Which of the following contain(s) tools for creating a document?
   a. tool panel
   b. tool bar
   c. tool menu
   d. all of the above

8. Which of the following options exits ClarisWorks?
   a. exit
   b. quit
   c. end
   d. stop

9. Which of the following must be done first when saving a document?
   a. identify the disk
   b. identify the file
   c. identify the computer
   d. none of the above

10. The process of saving a document differs from one application to another.
    a. true
    b. false

Applications

1. Write a letter to the parents of a student. In the letter, be sure to include a discussion of a subject at which the student is doing well. Then describe a subject at which the student is not doing as well. Make recommendations about how the parents may help their child with school work.

2. Before saving and printing the previous letter, go back and edit the letter to make it as positive as possible. Move the insertion point using the mouse and the arrow keys. Practice changing the attributes of selected text. Do not boldface, italicize, or underline too much text. It will make the document look too cluttered. Save and print the letter.

3. Develop a list of concepts, commands, definitions, or terms important to you that were presented in Chapters 1 and 2 of this text. Save the document and print it if you wish.

3

WORD PROCESSING ESSENTIALS

OBJECTIVES

Learning the material in this chapter will enable you to:

- enter text in the word processing portion of ClarisWorks
- use the word wrap feature
- edit text
- select blocks of text
- move, copy, and delete blocks of text
- save your documents
- use a variety of formatting features
- identify and use various type, paragraph, and page characteristics
- print your document
- retrieve a document from disk
- use the spell checker and thesaurus

OVERVIEW

Word processing is the one computer application that nearly everyone will find useful. Because all of us write, we all are able to benefit from learning to use a word processor.

Word processors allow users to perform four fundamental tasks—enter, edit, format, and print text. While there are many types of word processors available, each one performs these same four tasks. Certainly, word processors differ in how they complete these tasks. Some word processors offer only a few features, making them very easy to learn, but are difficult to use to create a full range of documents. Other word processors have many features for creating complex documents, but they may take years to fully learn. ClarisWorks provides a balance between these simple and complex word processors. ClarisWorks is easy to learn, yet has most of the features needed by the majority of word processor users.

The goal of this chapter is to teach you the fundamentals of using the word processing component of ClarisWorks. However, the goal goes much beyond simply learning which keys to press. Truly learning about word processing means focusing on the four major components of any word processor. By learning both which keys to press and how each concept relates to the creation of a quality document, you will be able to take your knowledge of ClarisWorks and apply it to virtually any other word processing program. This makes ClarisWorks the ideal learning tool. It is a great word processor in its own right. It is also a learning tool that will enable you to use virtually any other word processing program.

ENTERING TEXT

In the previous chapter you were provided a quick introduction to creating a word processing document with ClarisWorks. Now that you have seen how easy it is to create, save, and print a document in ClarisWorks, it's time to more fully examine the word processor.

Word processing begins with entering text. A word processor is not a typewriter, because the processes for entering and editing text differ from a typewriter. When you were in the fifth grade, your teacher probably asked you to write an essay in pencil, edit the essay in pencil, then re-write the entire document, neatly, in pen. What most of us actually learned was to try to create a final version while writing the first draft. The reason was simple—it took too much time to re-write the entire essay. With ClarisWorks, there is no need to be so precise when entering text, because the word processor makes editing so easy. Therefore, the first rule of word processing is to be unconcerned about initial technical accuracy, focusing instead on the flow of ideas. In other words, enter ideas first; you can easily fix grammatical and spelling errors, and make other changes later.

As mentioned, the insertion point is the most critical element when entering text into a ClarisWorks document. All text typed from the keyboard or imported from other sources is placed at the location of the insertion point. Therefore, the first step in entering text into a document is to place the insertion point at the desired location. Normally, you begin a document by placing the insertion point in the upper left corner of the column guides.

Once the insertion point is in the desired location, the next step is to type—to express the ideas onscreen. Again, do not be overly concerned with making sure every word is correctly spelled or that the document looks nice. It is easy to fix this later.

Word Wrap

Entering text with ClarisWorks differs from typing text on a standard typewriter. On a standard typewriter, the Return key ends each line and moves the carriage to the beginning of the next line. With ClarisWorks, it is not necessary for you to press the Enter key at the end of each line within a paragraph. Instead, ClarisWorks automatically moves the insertion point to the beginning of the next line as you type to the right edge of the margin. This process is called *word wrap*. Note that this is only for lines within a paragraph. To end a paragraph and force the insertion point to begin a new line requires pressing the Enter key.

Hands-On

1. Start ClarisWorks and create a new word processing document.

2. Make sure the insertion point is located in the upper left corner of the column guides.

3. Type the following. See Figure 3-1.

   Dear Mom: [Enter]

   [Enter]

   I regret to inform you that my last semester's grades were not up to either of our expectations. As the Dean of Students has informed me, I am on a record-setting pace for the lowest GPA in the history of this esteemed institution. I hope this news is not a shock. If I pass this computer class, I may be allowed to stay in school. If not, please have my old room ready for my return. [Enter]

   [Enter]

   Best Wishes [Enter]

4. Notice that there are only five locations where you press [Enter] within the document.

FIGURE 3-1

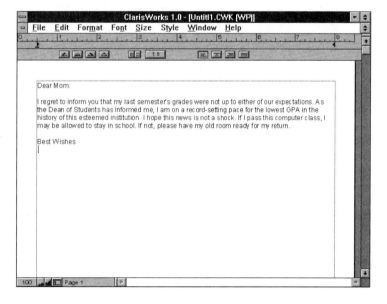

EDITING TEXT

Of course, the real strength of word processing is the ability to easily edit text. The basic editing processes occur when entering new text or deleting existing text. To enter new text, you must first move the insertion point to the location at which you wish the new text to appear. Once the insertion point is at the desired location, the next step is to type new text. All text entered at the location of the insertion point is inserted into the document, causing all existing text to shift to the right. In other words, text is "squeezed" into the location of the insertion point.

Deleting erases or removes text from a document. With Claris-Works, the easiest way to delete small amounts of text is to place the insertion point just to the right of what you want to delete, then press the Backspace key—go one space beyond and delete back. You can also use the Del or Delete key to delete one character to the right.

Inserting and deleting text is fine for small changes. However, for changing larger amounts of text, there is the process known as *blocking*. A *block* is a set of text within the document. Imagine having to delete five pages of text using the Backspace key—it would take a long time. However, by blocking a selected group of text, say five pages, you can delete the block by simply pressing one key.

Blocking and Deleting

Blocking is used for both editing and formatting text. ClarisWorks permits changes in text attributes to the entire document or changes to attributes for a selected block of text. For example, a block of text can be selected for single-spacing, double-spacing, moving, printing, indenting, or changing the overall appearance.

Blocking involves the process called *click and drag*—to move the I-beam to the beginning of the text to be selected, then drag it to the end of what you want to select. A block is marked by *inverse* text; in other words, white characters on a black or colored background.

You can turn off a block by clicking the mouse button any-where on the page. If you block the incorrect text, you can always try again. You may also modify the block in any number of ways.

One of the most important is deleting. To delete blocked text, press the delete key. For those nervous about deleting a large block of text, ClarisWorks offers the Undo Typing and Redo Typing options in the Edit menu. Immediately after you delete a block of text, you may return the text to the insertion point by selecting Undo Typing from the Edit menu. Redo Typing allows you to re-delete the block of text.

Hands-On

1. Move the I-beam to the beginning of *Dear Mom:*.

2. Click and hold down the mouse button, then drag the I-beam just to the right of *Mom:*. Now release the mouse button.

   You have blocked *Dear Mom:*. See Figure 3-2.

FIGURE 3-2

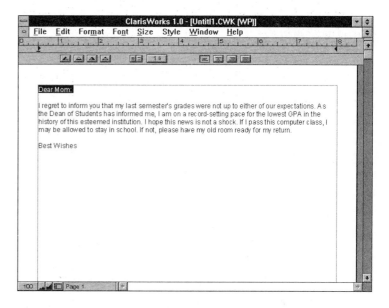

3. If you were not successful with step two try again.

    From this point on, we'll use the verbs *block* and *select* interchangeably. For example, "Select *Dear Mom:*" means to create a block with the text *Dear Mom:*.

4. Select *Mom.* See if you can do it without selecting the colon.

5. With *Mom* selected, press (Del)

    The selected text is removed. See Figure 3-3.

6. Now insert *Dad* where *Mom* used to be.

FIGURE 3-3

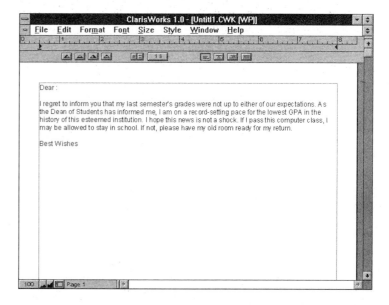

Edit
<u>U</u>ndo Typing	Ctrl+Z
Cu<u>t</u>	Ctrl+X
<u>C</u>opy	Ctrl+C
<u>P</u>aste	Ctrl+V
Cl<u>e</u>ar	
Select <u>A</u>ll	Ctrl+A
Insert <u>D</u>ate	
Insert Ti<u>m</u>e	
Insert Page #	
<u>S</u>pelling	▶
<u>F</u>ind/Change	▶
P<u>r</u>eferences...	

FIGURE 3-4

7. Select *Dad* and delete the block.

8. Choose the Undo Typing option from the Edit menu shown in Figure 3-4.

9. The deleted text returns to the location of the insertion point.

10. Select Redo Typing from the Edit menu.

11. Notice the selected text is deleted again.

Exercise 3-1 Practice inserting and deleting text. Be sure to experiment with Undo Typing and Redo Typing. However, do not save changes to the letter's content. This will make the next section easier to follow. You can change the contents of this letter a bit later.

MOVING AND COPYING TEXT

One of the real strengths of blocking is the ease with which you can copy or move blocks of text. For example, if you want to make the first paragraph of a document the second paragraph, it is much easier to block and move the paragraph than it is to delete the first paragraph and retype the paragraph in a new location.

Three menu commands are used in this process—Cut, Copy, and Paste, all under the Edit menu. Selecting Cut removes the block of text from the document and places it in the Clipboard, a special temporary location. Copy places the block of text in the Clipboard, but also leaves the text in its original location. Paste retrieves the text from the Clipboard and places it at the insertion point. Once text is in the Clipboard, it may be retrieved by using the Paste option. This allows you to place a block of text at several locations within a document.

 *Hands-On*

1. From the letter to Mom and Dad, select the sentence— *I hope this news is not a shock.* See Figure 3-5.

2. Select the Cut option from the Edit menu.

   The sentence disappears from the document.

3. Place the insertion point at the beginning of the paragraph, then select Paste from the Edit menu.

   Notice the result, shown in Figure 3-6.

FIGURE 3-5

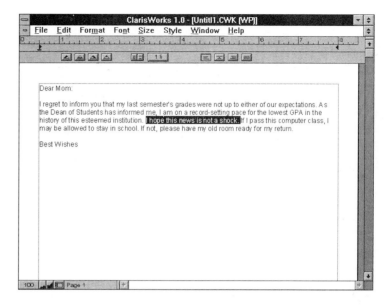

4. You may need to insert or delete a space depending on how you selected the block. It is common to make minor adjustments to a document after using Cut, Copy, or Paste.

FIGURE 3-6

Exercise 3-2   Practice. Rearrange the contents of your document by using Cut, Copy, and Paste. Be sure to use Copy to place a sentence in more than one location.

Saving

Saving is, of course, critical. In Chapter 2 you were introduced to the save process. Here is a quick step-by-step review.

Hands-On

1. Since this is a new document, select Save As from the File menu. This produces the Save As dialog box shown in Figure 3-7.

2. Click on the box below Drives to obtain a list of available drives.

3. Select A: or the drive you are using.

   Notice that the contents of Drives: is A:.

4. Delete UNTITL1.CWK and type MOMLTR.CWK, as shown in Figure 3-8.

5. Click on OK.

6. From now on, every time you want to save this document, you only need select Save from the File menu. Claris-Works will save the document to the correct drive and directory.

FIGURE 3-7

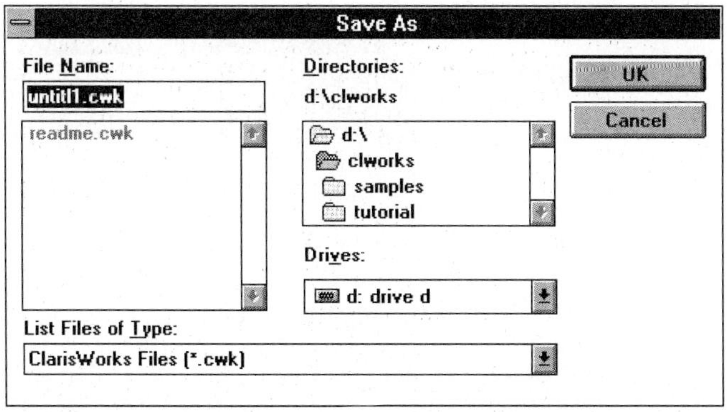

FIGURE 3-8

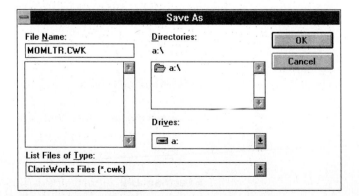

FORMATTING TEXT

At this point, you should be able to create, edit, and save a document to disk. You have focused on the content of the document, not on changing the presentation of text. Word processing software not only makes it easy to focus on content, it allows you to consider the elements of visual presentation. ClarisWorks provides numerous tools for setting the presentation of a document. Setting a document's presentation is known as *formatting* text.

The key to formatting text is the block function. As with editing, blocking allows you to select a group of text within a document. In formatting, you select text to change some style attribute of that text.

Type Characteristics

The formatting adjustments to text fall within one of three major categories—typeface, typestyle, and typesize. The *typeface* is the design of type. *Typeface* is used interchangeably with the term *font* to indicate all sizes of type with the same design.

Depending on the configuration of your computer, ClarisWorks may have several different typefaces. These are available as options under the Font menu. You may use any of the fonts that are available in the Font menu for any or all text within your document. Just select the text you want to change, then select the font.

When many fonts are available, it is important to use them appropriately. There are two major font types—serif and sans serif. Serif fonts are those with little extension lines at the letters' ends. Sans serif type lacks those lines. The text sections of this book are printed in a serif font, and the Hands-on sections are printed in a sans serif font. The selection of font depends on the message. In general, the major body of text is printed in serif typefaces to make reading easier. Sans serif faces work well for titles and headings that stand out from the rest of the text. However, sometimes a sans serif typeface is appropriate for the body of text, and serif fonts sometimes work well as titles. As a general rule, never use more than two fonts in any one document.

Typesize refers to the size of the letters. Typesize is measured in points, from very small (two points) to very large (128 points or even larger). As a general rule, 10- and 12-point type are used for the body of the text, with larger sizes used for titles and subtitles, and smaller sizes used for footnotes and quotations.

As with selecting a font, choosing a size is as simple as selecting a group of text, then choosing the desired size from the Size menu.

Typestyle refers to variations of type within a typeface or font. Examples of typestyles include plain text, bold, italic, underline, subscript, and superscript. For most applications, the three most common styles are plain text, bold, and italic.

1. Add your name and address to the upper left-hand corner of your document.

2. Select your name.

3. Choose 24 point from the Size menu.

    Notice the results. See Figure 3-9.

4. With your name still selected, choose Helvetica from the Font menu. If this font is not available, select another.

5. Select all lines that contain your address.

6. Choose the Helvetica-Narrow font. If this font is not available, select another.

    Notice the results.

7. Select all remaining text within your document and set the text to 12 point Times. See Figure 3-10.

8. Select the word *regret* in the document's first sentence.

9. Choose 14 point from the Size menu, then select Bold from the Style menu.

FIGURE 3-8

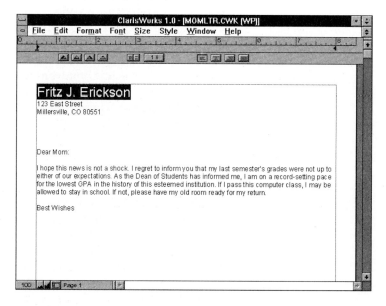

Exercise 3-3   Experiment now with the many different type attributes available within ClarisWorks. Be sure to save your document after completing this exercise (use the Save option in the File menu).

Paragraph Characteristics

In addition to setting attributes for selected text, ClarisWorks provides a number of options for controlling the appearance of paragraphs. The overall appearance of a document is set with the icons below the ruler.

FIGURE 3-10

As with setting type characteristics, there are two steps for setting paragraph characteristics. First, you must select the paragraph. Second, you assign the attribute. Selecting a paragraph is done differently than selecting a block. To select a paragraph, just place the insertion point anywhere within the desired paragraph. If you wish to select more than one paragraph, you must use the same blocking technique used with assigning text attributes.

Alignment   Setting paragraph alignment is an important part of determining the overall appearance of a document. There are four types of alignment—left, center, right, and justified.

Alignment is set by using one of the four alignment icons below the ruler. The left option causes a paragraph to align smoothly on the left margin while leaving text ragged on the right. The right option is the opposite—smooth right, but ragged left. Center causes all text within the paragraph to center within the margins. Finally, justified means that text is aligned smoothly along both the right and left margins.

Because setting alignment is so common, ClarisWorks provides four alignment icons just below the ruler. To select any of these four alignment settings, simply put the insertion point within the desired paragraph and click on the desired alignment icon. If you want to set the alignment for the entire document, you can use the Select All option in the Edit menu to select all text and paragraphs.

1. Place the insertion point within the main paragraph of your letter.

2. Click on the center icon (second from the left).

   The results are shown in Figure 3-11.

FIGURE 3-11

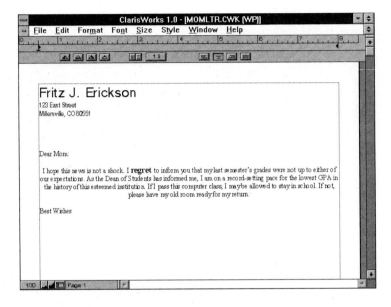

3. Select each of the other three alignment icons to see the results. Be sure to return the paragraph to left alignment.

Indent and Tab   Indent and tab are options that place spaces within a paragraph. There are three indent options within Claris-Works. You can indent an entire paragraph from the left or right. You can indent the first line of a paragraph. Finally, you can outdent the first line of a paragraph. Tab is a keystroke placed within a paragraph that corresponds to a tab setting on the ruler. By default, Claris-Works has set all tabs at half inches. In other words, each tab stops at half-inch increments on the ruler. The difference between a tab and an indent is that indent moves the entire paragraph, while tab affects only an individual line.

To indent a paragraph from either the left or right, you must use the indent setting on the ruler. This is done with the ruler's small triangles. The left indent triangle is located on the left margin. To set the indent, first select the paragraph, then click on and drag the indent triangle to any location on the ruler. The left indent cannot exceed the right indent nor the right margin.

If you want to indent only the first line of a paragraph, there are two choices. First, you may insert a tab at the beginning of the desired paragraph. Second, you may use the First line indent option. On the ruler, the First line indent option is an inverse T located below the Left indent mark. By clicking and dragging this mark to a new location, you can set the first line indent.

Setting tabs at different locations than the half-inch default is done by dragging the tab setting icons located below the ruler to a desired location on the ruler. There are four tab setting icons available—left, right, center, and align on.

Hands-On

1. Select the main paragraph in your letter.

2. Click and hold on the left indent mark on the ruler, located just above the left column guide.

3. Drag the indent mark to the three-inch point on the ruler and release the mouse button.

   The entire paragraph is indented two and one-half inches. See Figure 3-12.

4. Below the left indent mark is the first line indent mark. Drag this to the four-inch ruler point and release the mouse button. (This may take a bit of practice.)

   Notice the effect of this setting, shown in Figure 3-13.

FIGURE 3-12

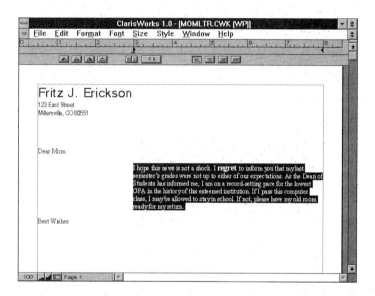

FIGURE 3-13

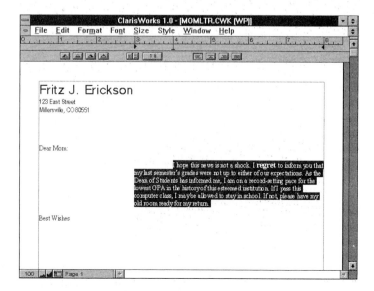

5. Return the left indent and first line indent mark to one and one-half inches.

6. Click and hold on the left tab mark and drag it to the two-inch point on the ruler. Release the mouse button and notice that the tab mark now appears within the ruler, as shown in Figure 3-14.

7. From the keyboard, insert a tab in the main paragraph.

    Notice the location of the tab.

8. To remove the tab, click on the two-inch tab mark and drag it back to the left tab icon, then release the mouse button.

    Notice that the tab mark is removed from the ruler and the tab setting returns to the default half-inch setting.

FIGURE 3-14

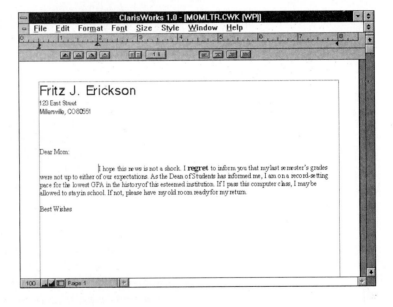

Line spacing Setting paragraph line spacing is done by using line spacing icons. Most line spacing is set either to single or double. However, you can have greater than double spacing or increments, such as one and one-half, if you choose.

To set line spacing, select the desired paragraph(s), then click the line spacing icon. This icon has three components. The first decreases the line spacing by half of a line. The second increases the line spacing by half. The third displays the current line space setting.

1. With the main paragraph of this document selected, click once on the middle portion of the line spacing icon. This will increase the line spacing by one-half inch.

2. Click again and notice the results.

3. Reduce the line spacing by clicking on the right portion of this icon.

Page Characteristics

The third group of format settings involves changing the layout of text and the overall appearance of the page. ClarisWorks provides a host of page setup options. Those discussed in this chapter include Margins, Columns, Page Breaks, Page Numbers, and Headers and Footers.

Margins Margins determine where all text will appear on a page relative to the edge of the paper. The column guides appear on-screen at the locations of the left and right margins. The way to modify the margins is with the Document option in the Format menu.

There are four margin settings—top, bottom, left, and right. As long as the margins do not overlap, you may set them to anything you want. However, the margin settings should be appropriate to the type of document you are creating and the page size, which is determined through the Page Setup option in the File menu. Available page sizes are limited by the capacity of the printer connected to your computer.

It does not matter where the insertion point is when setting margins.

1. Select Document from the Format menu.

2. Set all margins to one inch. See Figure 3-15.

3. Click on OK and notice the results.

4. Change the margins back to one-half inch.

FIGURE 3-15

Document	
Margins	**Display**
Top: `1`	⦿ 🖹 ◯ 🖺 ◯ `3`
Bottom: `1`	☒ Show **M**argins
Left: `1`	☒ Show Page **G**uides
Right: `1`	☐ Title **P**age
Starting Page #: `1`	Cancel OK

Columns ClarisWorks allows you to design a multiple-column page by selecting the desired number of columns through the Columns option of the Format menu. In addition to setting the number of columns, you may alter the distance between columns. Claris-Works will automatically calculate the width of each column based on the margin settings and the specified space between columns.

Hands-On

1. Choose the Columns option from the Format menu.

2. Press 2 to set the number of columns in your letter to two. See Figure 3-16.

3. Click on OK and notice the results, shown in Figure 3-17.

4. Return the document to a single-column design.

FIGURE 3-16

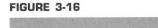

Columns

Number of: 2

Space Between: 0.17 in

Cancel   OK

FIGURE 3-17

ClarisWorks 1.0 - [MOMLTR.CWK (WP)]

File Edit Format Font Size Style Window Help

Fritz J. Erickson

123 East Street
Millersville, CO 60551

Dear Mom:

I hope this news is not a shock. I **regret** to inform you that my last semester's grades were not up to either of our expectations. As the Dean of Students has informed me, I am on a record-setting pace for the lowest GPA in the history of this esteemed institution. If I pass this computer class, I may be allowed to stay in school. If not, please have my old room ready for my return.

Best Wishes

100   Page 1

Headers and footers A header is the words placed at the top of every page. A footer is the words placed at the bottom of every page. Headers and footers help organize word processing documents. For example, a term paper may have the author's name and a brief title of the paper on every page. Headers and footers may also contain page numbers, current date, and time.

To create a header or footer, select Insert Header or Insert Footer from the Format menu. After selecting one or both of these, the header or footer location appears within a separate set of column guides on the page. Once these appear, you may insert text and assign any attribute to the text. You may even press the enter key to expand the size of the header or footer. Every page of the document will print the contents of the header or footer.

One of the most important pieces of information to include in a header or footer are page numbers. To place a page number within a header or a footer, first place the insertion point within the header or footer, then select Insert Page # from the Edit menu. The correct page number will appear. Remember, a header or footer is like any other paragraph, and you can change the alignment, type, or paragraph attribute.

 *Hands-On*

1. Select Insert Header from the Format Menu.

   The header area appears within the document.

2. Move the I-beam inside the header and click to place the insertion point.

3. Choose Insert Page # from the Edit menu.

   Notice the page number appears. See Figure 3-18.

4. Set the alignment for this paragraph to right to force the page number to align along the right margin.

5. Insert the word *Page* followed by a space before the page number.

FIGURE 3-18

ClarisWorks 1.0 - [MOMLTR.CWK [WP]]

File Edit Format Font Size Style Window Help

Fritz J. Erickson
123 East Street
Millersville, CO 80551

Dear Mom:

I hope this news is not a shock. I **regret** to inform you that my last semester's grades were not up to either of our expectations. As the Dean of Students has informed me, I am on a record-setting pace for the lowest GPA in the history of this esteemed institution. If I pass this computer class, I may be allowed to stay in school. If not, please have my old room ready for my return.

Best Wishes

6. To the left of Page 1, type your name, then press [Tab] .

    Because the tab is a left tab, your name will move to the left edge of the header, as shown in Figure 3-19.

7. After the 1, press [Enter] to insert a blank line.

FIGURE 3-19

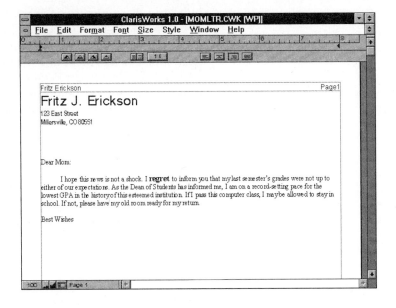

Page breaks When entering more text than will fit on a single page, ClarisWorks automatically inserts page breaks relative to the bottom margin. However, there are occasions when you want to insert a page break to split text to two different pages. For example, after entering text for a title page, it is appropriate to insert a page break so the remaining text will begin at the top of the second page.

Inserting a page break into a document first requires that you put the insertion point where you want the page to break. After placing the insertion point, select Insert Break from the Format menu. Separate pages will appear within the window for every page of a document.

Deleting a page break is done the same way as deleting any other text within a document. First, put the insertion point one space beyond the page break, which is always at the very top of the new page. Next, press the Backspace key.

Hands-On

1. Place the insertion point after *Dear Dad:*.

2. Select Insert Break from the Format menu.

    Notice that the text moves to a new page, and the Pages at the bottom of the screen changes to 1-2 as shown in Figure 3-20.

FIGURE 3-20

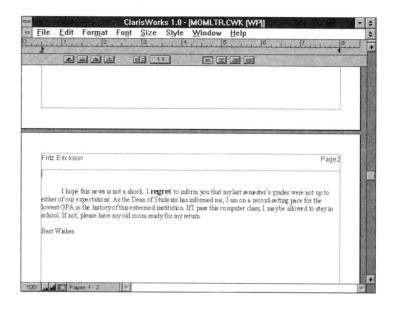

3. Place the insertion point at the top of page two, then press (Backspace)

    This deletes the page break and returns the document to one page.

Exercise 3-4   It's time to change your MOMLTR.CWK document. Alter both the style and content of this letter. Make the letter as presentable as possible and be sure to save it on your disk.

PRINTING TEXT

The final step in creating a word processing document is to print. Printing was discussed in the previous chapter and is reviewed here.

To print a document, you simply select the Print option from the File menu. This produces the Print dialog box. This dialog box is important because it specifies the printer, the number of copies, and which pages to print. These are the three most important settings; however, you may have several other controls, depending on your printer.

The printer listed at the top of the Print dialog box must match the printer connected to the computer. If not, you must select Cancel in this dialog box and consult with your instructor or lab technician. Once the correct printer is displayed, the next step is to determine the number of copies and which pages to print. If All is selected under Print Range, all pages within the document will be sent to the printer. You may also specify pages with the From: and To: options.

One final note. Always save your document before printing. Printing sometimes causes a wide range of problems, including locking your computer. If this happens, you will need to reboot the computer, thereby removing your document from memory. If the document is saved on disk, it is easy to recall.

1. Just to be sure, select Save from the File menu to save MOMLTR.CWK.

2. Select Print from the File menu.

    This produces the Print dialog box shown in Figure 3-21.

3. Make sure the printer name at the top of this dialog box is correct.

4. Print one copy of all pages by clicking on the Print button.

5. Select Exit from the File menu to exit ClarisWorks.

FIGURE 3-21

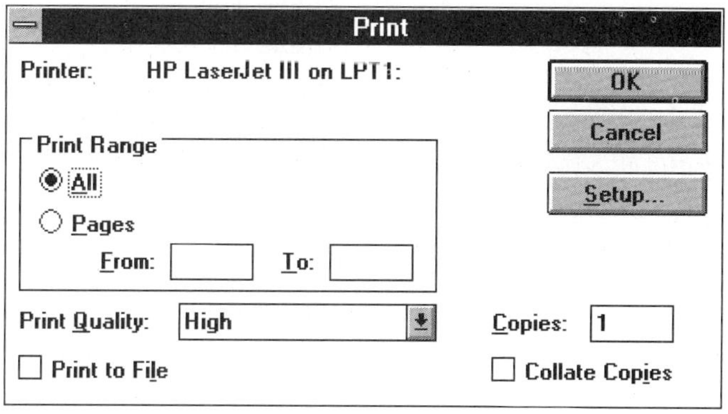

Print	
Printer: HP LaserJet III on LPT1:	

Print Range
◉ **A**ll
○ **P**ages
  From: ☐   **T**o: ☐

Print **Q**uality: High ▼

☐ Print to Fi**l**e

OK
Cancel
Setup...

Copies: 1

☐ Collate Cop**i**es

RETRIEVING DOCUMENTS

Now that you have created, edited, formatted, saved, and printed a document, the last task is to retrieve a document from a disk for additional editing. When you start ClarisWorks, the New Document dialog box appears. If you wish to use an existing document rather than create a new document, you must select Cancel to terminate this dialog box. To open an existing document, you must select Open from the File menu. This will produce a dialog box for retrieving your word processing document.

The Open dialog box allows you to retrieve a document. First, select the location where the document resides. Second, select the appropriate document and file type. Third, select the desired file name from the list of files. The List Files of Type option is typically set to ClarisWorks files (*.cwk).

Once the desired file appears in the file list, simply double click on the desired file name. Double clicking has the same effect as clicking once on the file name, then clicking on the Open button. In a few moments your file appears with the file name in the window title bar. Since the file was open, ClarisWorks knows both the file name and file location. You may save the document again by using the Save option in the File menu, rather than using Save As.

Hands-On

1. Start ClarisWorks.

2. At the New Document dialog box, click on Cancel.

3. Select Open from the File menu.

4. Select Drive A: and notice the file list of all files on the A: drive with the .CWK extension.

   The document MOMLTR.CWK should appear, along with any other ClarisWorks files, in the file list. See Figure 3-22.

5. Double click on MOMLTR.CWK.

   This opens the document.

FIGURE 3-22

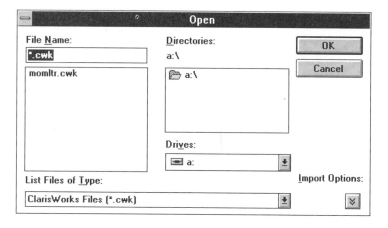

ADDITIONAL FEATURES

Two of the most popular features of powerful word processors such as ClarisWorks are the spell checker and thesaurus. These tools are both editing tools and writing tools. Of course, making sure the spelling of words within a document is correct is an important part of editing. But a spell checker can also free you from worrying about spelling, thereby freeing you to focus on expression in writing. The thesaurus searches for and lists synonyms. Using the thesaurus can help improve your writing.

Spell Check

For many people, a key reason for using a word processor is its ability to check the spelling of a document against an electronic dictionary. The spell checker compares each word in a document to a list of words in an electronic dictionary. If a word in the document does not match any word in the dictionary, the spell checker identifies the word as a possible misspelling. Once a word has been identified, you have several options. You may identify the word as correctly spelled, edit the word, or choose a word from a list of possible correctly spelled words.

As with any word processor, the spell check feature does not guarantee correctness. Because the spell checker checks only spelling, not meaning, it cannot identify mistakes in the use of homonyms. For example, using *weather* for *whether* will not be identified as a mistake. In addition, proper nouns are not part of most dictionaries (although you may add proper names and other words to the dictionary).

Using the spell checker in ClarisWorks begins by selecting the Spelling option from the Edit menu. There are three spelling options, including Check Document, which checks the spelling of the entire document. Other options include Install Dictionaries and User Dictionaries.

When ClarisWorks is first installed, two types of dictionaries are automatically created—a main dictionary and a user dictionary. The main dictionary contains thousands of words and is the basis for the spell check program. However, it may not contain words peculiar to specialties. The user dictionary enables you to create a specialized dictionary. For example, you may wish to create a dictionary containing scientific terms for biology. You may choose or create user dictionaries at any time. For now, however, focus only on the main dictionary.

To use the spell checker with the main dictionary, simply select Spelling from the Edit menu, and select the Check Document option. The spell checker will compare every word in your document to all words in the main dictionary. When a possibly mispelled word is encountered, a window appears identifying the word in question and lists suggested spellings. To replace a word with one of the suggested spellings, all you need do is click on the desired spelling, then click on Replace. If the identified word is correctly spelled (for example, if it is a proper noun), you click on Skip to accept that spelling. The Learn button enables you to add the identified word to the user dictionary.

In some situations, the word identified is so misspelled that ClarisWorks cannot offer even one suggestion. In other situations, the word is incorrectly spelled, but a correct spelling does not appear in the list of suggestions. In either of these cases, you may correct the word directly in the Word: box. After correcting the word, clicking on the Check button rechecks the newly-entered word against the dictionary. Even if the word is still misspelled, Claris-Works may be able to offer some suggestions.

Hands-On

1. Make sure your MOMLTR.CWK document is onscreen.

2. Change the word *expectations* to the incorrect spelling *expecations.*

3. Select Spelling from the Edit menu.

   This produces three spelling options, shown in Figure 3-23.

4. Select Check Document.

   The word *expecations* is incorrect, causing the Spelling window to appear with *expecations* next to Word:, and one suggestion appears beneath. See Figure 3-24.

5. Because there is only one suggestion, click on Replace.

   Notice that the spell checker continues through the document. Once it is finished, be sure to save the corrected document on disk. Spelling changes are no different from any other form of editing—you must save these changes.

FIGURE 3-23

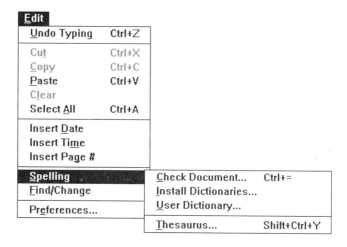

FIGURE 3-24

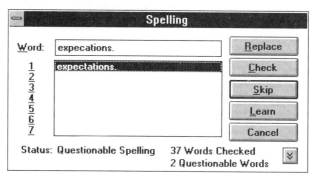

Exercise 3-5   Check the spelling of all the documents you have created thus far. From now on, there should be no reason for any spelling mistake in any file. You may have usage mistakes, such as *weather* for *whether,* but at least the usage mistake is correctly spelled.

Thesaurus

The thesaurus lists synonyms for selected words to help you avoid overusing words or to find words that more precisely express a meaning. The first step in using the thesaurus is to select one word within the document. This, of course, is done by blocking. Activate the thesaurus through the Spelling option of the Edit menu. This produces a list of words for your consideration. If you find a word that you would like to use, click on it, then click on the Replace button. If you do not find a word and want to expand your search, you may select any word within the list, then click on Lookup. This will create a new list of words.

 *Hands-On*

1. With MOMLTR.CWK onscreen, select the word *regret* (refer to Figure 3-25). If you do not have *regret,* pick another word.

2. Select the Spelling option from the Edit menu, then choose Thesaurus.

   Notice that *regret* appears next to Find:, and a list of synonyms appears above. See Figure 3-26.

3. Scroll down the list to the verbs, click on *apologize,* then click on Replace.

   Apologize now appears within the document. Of course, this does not make sense, so use the Thesaurus again to find another word that works.

FIGURE 3-25

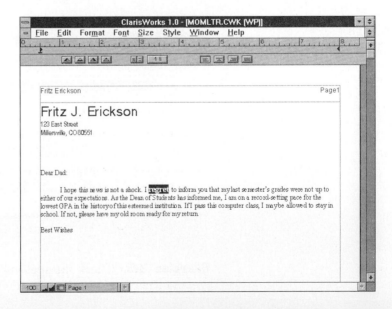

FIGURE 3-26

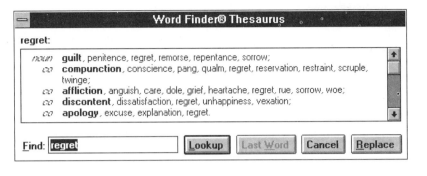

Summary

- When entering text, the most important point is to put ideas into words and concentrate on the content of a document.

- Word processors, by definition, allow users to perform four fundamental tasks—enter text, edit text, format text, and print.

- All text typed from the keyboard or imported from other sources is placed at the location of the insertion point.

- ClarisWorks automatically moves the insertion point to the beginning of the next line in a paragraph as you type through the right edge of the screen. This is called *word wrap.*

- A block is a subset of text within the document.

- Blocking involves dragging.

- Immediately after you delete a block of text, you may return the text to the insertion point by selecting Undo Typing from the Edit menu.

- Cut removes the block of text from the document and places it in a special temporary location known as the Clipboard.

- Copy places the block of text in the Clipboard, but also leaves the text in its original location.

- Paste retrieves the text from the Clipboard and places it within the document at the location of the insertion point.

- The tools for adjusting the appearance of text fall within one of three major categories—typeface, typestyle, and typesize.

- A typeface identifies the design of type. It is used interchangeably with the term *font* to indicate all sizes of type with the same appearance.

- As a general rule, never use more than two fonts in any one document.

■ Typesize refers to the size of characters measured in points.

■ Typestyle refers to variations of type within a typeface or font.

■ There are four types of alignment—left, center, right, and justified.

■ Margins determine where all text will appear on a page relative to edge of the paper.

■ ClarisWorks allows you to design a multiple-column page by selecting the desired number of columns through the Columns option of the Format menu.

■ A header is a few words placed at the top of every page. A footer is a few words placed at the bottom of every page.

■ Always save your document before printing.

■ The Open dialog box allows you to retrieve a document by selecting the location where the document resides, selecting the appropriate document and file type, and selecting the desired file name from the list of files.

■ The spell checker compares each word in a document to a list of words in an electronic dictionary.

■ The thesaurus lists synonyms for selected words to help you avoid overusing words or to find words that more precisely express a meaning.

Questions

1. The term _Blocking_ generally refers to the text that has been selected for change.

2. A small symbol, such as a flashing line or box, usually indicates the location of the _insertion point_ .

3. The procedures for setting margins, line spacing, and setting headers and footers are called _page set up_ procedures.

4. To end a paragraph and force the insertion point to begin a new line requires using the _Enter_ key.

5. With ClarisWorks, the easiest way to delete small amounts of text is to place the insertion point just to the _left_ of what you want to delete, then press the _Del_ key.

6. Selecting _cut_ removes the block of text from the document and places it in a special temporary location known as the _clipboard_ .

7. As a general rule, never use more than ___2___ fonts in any one document.

8. ___Typestyle___ refers to variations of type within a typeface or font.

9. When you enter more text than can fit on a single page, ClarisWorks automatically inserts ___page Breaks___ .

10. The ___Thesaurus___ provides you the tool for finding synonyms.

Quiz

1. A spelling checker will not check for the use of correctly spelled but misused homonyms.
    a. true   b. false

2. The term point means:
    a. the exact location of type   b. the size of type
    c. the amount of space   d. the appearance of large
       required for certain text   type

3. Which of the following causes text to automatically flow from one line of a paragraph to the next line within the same paragraph?
    a. word wrap   b. text wrap
    c. character wrap   d. flow wrap

4. With almost any activity, the first step is to:
    a. select text   b. place the insertion point
    c. click and drag   d. select menu items

5. Blocking involves the process of:
    a. double clicking   b. clicking and releasing
    c. clicking and dragging   d. selecting text

6. Once you select a block, you must assign a text attribute.
    a. true   b. false

7. Which of the following leaves the original block in the document?
    a. Cut   b. Copy
    c. Paste   d. Clipboard

8. There is no difference between Save and Save As.
    a. true   b. false

9. Where should page numbers print?
    a. at the top of a page   b. at the bottom of a page
    c. within a header or footer   d. on every page of a document

10. Which type of alignment causes text to align smoothly along the right *and* left margins?
    a. right
    b. left
    c. center
    (d.) justified

Applications

1. One of the most useful applications of word processing is to write your résumé. Use ClarisWorks to create a visually appealing résumé. This résumé should reflect as much about you as possible yet still be concise. You may want to visit your college or university placement office for some useful tips.

2. Write a business letter to Santa Claus. This should be a formal letter that is both direct and informative. Pick a font that helps convey this formality and use a writing style to enhance your message. Be sure to print a copy of your letter and save your letter on disk.

3. Write an informal letter to a friend. This letter should be light and fun to read. You may want to select one or more fonts to help convey a friendly message. Again, print a copy of your letter and save it on your disk.

SPREADSHEET ESSENTIALS

OBJECTIVES

Learning the material in this chapter will enable you to:

- describe the purpose of spreadsheet software
- describe how ClarisWorks creates worksheets
- describe how a worksheet organizes data
- list the major data types
- describe the process of entering data into a worksheet
- define data formats
- describe the calculation options
- define absolute and relative cell address
- define print options
- describe how to use charts for data presentation

OVERVIEW

The second most popular application in ClarisWorks is the spreadsheet. Just as word processors make it easier to work with words, spreadsheets make it easier to work with numbers. In fact, spreadsheets are often called word processors for numbers because of the techniques for entering, editing, formatting, and printing.

To help you understand how the ClarisWorks spreadsheet operates, you need to consider how this software organizes information. The primary organizational tool is called a *worksheet*, which is similar to an electronic grid. Within the spreadsheet software, each grid of data is called a worksheet. In each worksheet are locations called *cells*. Cells store information and are identified by row and column. Cells may contain numbers, but they may also contain formulas for mathematical calculation and labels for identifying formulas and numbers.

The true strength of a spreadsheet is in its use of mathematical formulas. A formula manipulates numbers, referred to as *values*, contained in other cells. Changing a value in one of those other cells causes the formula to recalculate to account for the change. This very powerful feature allows you to ask the question "What If?" For example, what if you receive a 25 cent per hour raise? How much extra money would you take home each payday? With the spreadsheet application of ClarisWorks, you may place your old hourly pay in one cell, and in another cell enter the number of hours worked. In a third cell, you could write a formula to multiply the hourly rate by the number of hours worked. The cell with the formula would display your total wages. If you later add 25 cents to the hourly rate in the first cell, the cell with the formula will automatically display the new total wages. You could also ask how working more hours would affect your wages. A change in the cell containing the number of hours worked would also be automatically reflected in the cell displaying total wages. This is a simple example, but you can see that it is possible to ask several what if questions of spreadsheet programs and see the impact of the change almost immediately.

This chapter will help you better understand what a spreadsheet does and how to use the ClarisWorks spreadsheet. Be sure to spend time practicing many of the skills presented throughout this chapter.

SPREADSHEET ESSENTIALS

Suppose you need to develop and maintain a family budget. One approach to this task is to list all household expenses and sources of income, writing the word *balance* at the end of the list. Across the top of the page, you would write the name of each month. After setting this initial structure, you would place numbers for income and expenses for January, February, and so on. At the end of the column next to the word *balance* you would subtract the total expenses from the total income for each month.

One problem with this method of creating a family budget comes up when entering an incorrect expense or payment amount. Discovering such a mistake requires recalculating the balance. A second problem is the lack of flexibility. What if the family needs a new car? How large a monthly payment can they afford? Answering such questions means making many additional calculations. Spreadsheets are an alternative to creating a family budget on a piece of paper or an accounting sheet—they perform the same task more quickly, easily, and efficiently.

Rows, Columns, and Cells

When you start a new spreadsheet in ClarisWorks, a screen very different from the word processing application's screen appears. This screen is known as a *worksheet*—an electronic grid of rows (horizontal cells) and columns (vertical cells). Columns are lettered across the top of the worksheet. Rows are numbered down the left edge. A letter and number combination, the cell *address*, identifies each cell within the worksheet. For example, the first cell under column A in row 1 is cell A1. See Figure 4-1.

FIGURE 4-1

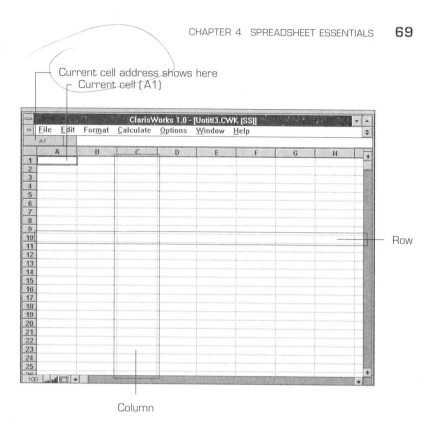

Current cell address shows here
Current cell (A1)

Row

Column

Cell Ranges

A cell name (for example, B3) refers to a single cell. Several cells in sequence are called a *range*. For example, the range from cell A1 to E1 represents five cells, all on row one. The range from cell A1 to A5 describes five cells in column A. ClarisWorks uses two dots (..) to indicate a cell range. For example, A1..A5 refers to the range of cells from A1 to A5. Figure 4-2 displays a cell range from B2 to B10. This is commonly referred to as a *block* of cells.

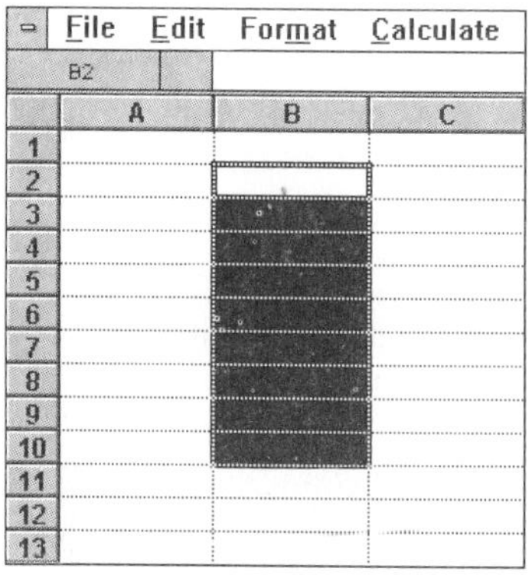

Current Cell

The current cell identifies the active cell for entering or editing worksheet data. The current cell is indicated by a dark or heavy border around the entire current cell. All data entered into a spreadsheet appears in the current cell. Therefore, the first step in entering data is to designate the current cell at the desired location. It is very important to check the location of the current cell before entering data. Probably the most common mistake made is to forget the current cell location and accidentally enter data into the wrong cell. Figure 4-3 shows cell C10 as the current cell.

Worksheets can consist of more than 150 columns and several thousand rows. Naturally, only a small area appears onscreen at any one time. This visible area is often referred to as the worksheet *window*. To view different areas of the worksheet, use the scroll bars to the left and bottom of the worksheet.

FIGURE 4-2

ᗕ	File	Edit	Format	Calculate	Options

	A	B	C	D
C10				

	A	B	C	D
1				
2				
3				
4				
5				
6				
7				
8				
9				
10				
11				
12				
13				

FIGURE 4-3

Spreadsheet Data

With word processing, there is only one type of data—text. However, the spreadsheet uses four primary types of data. Each type of data influences the type of operations that can be performed. These four basic types of data are labels, values, date and time, and formulas.

Labels   Labels are text entries that describe the contents of other cells. For example, in the household budget mentioned earlier, the income and expense categories and the months' names are labels. Labels may sometimes contain numbers—for example, social security numbers for employees—but labels cannot be part of a mathematical operation. That is, words cannot be added or subtracted.

Values   Values are numeric information, most commonly numbers. For example, the value 123 in cell B4 may be added, subtracted, multiplied, divided, squared, or used in almost any other mathematical operation with any other cell containing a value.

Date and time   Date and time data represent specific dates and times. They are entered in the form you type them but stored as a serial number. Date and time data can be used for comparisons, such as before 1/1/1995.

Formulas   Formulas are special types of values designed to manipulate data in cells that contain values. For example, a formula in cell N4 can automatically add the 12 monthly car payments in cells B4 through M4. The formula may look like this: =B4+C4+D4+E4+F4+G4+H4+I4+J4+K4+L4+M4. Formulas begin with a special character—here, an equal sign (=). The equal sign tells the worksheet program that what follows is not a label, it's a mathematical expression.

As mentioned earlier, the strength of a spreadsheet is in its use of formulas. A formula automatically performs the specified operation on the numeric contents of the specified cells, no matter how those values change. Suppose you want to know how an increase in your car payment—say, to $165.00—would affect the budget. Changing the values in cells B4..M4 to $165.00 would automatically cause the total in cell N4 to reflect this change.

Functions   A potential problem with entering formulas into cells is length. The formula =B4+C4+D4+E4+F4+G4+H4+I4+J4+K4+L4+M4 is fairly long. Imagine adding a series of 200 cells. Even if you don't mind typing long formulas, there is a character limit. To address this problem, spreadsheets have functions as alternatives to standard mathematical formulas.

Most functions identify specific operations by name and require a range of cells on which the operation will be performed.

For example, =SUM(A1:A5) is an addition function that totals the values in all cells beginning with A1 and ending with A5. The range of cells selected must not include the cell that contains the function. As with formulas, the equal sign marks the following letters as part of a function. Table 4-1 gives some examples of the functions available.

Table 4-1 Some Common Spreadsheet Functions

Function	Description
=AVERAGE(A1..A5)	Averages the values in cells A1 to A5
=SUM(A1..A5)	Totals the values in cells A1 to A5
=SQRT(x)	Finds the positive square root of x
=RAND	Generates a random number between zero and one
=VAR(A1:A5)	Finds the population variance of values in cells A1 to A5
=STDE(A1:A5)	Finds the standard deviation of the values in cells A1 to A5

ENTERING DATA

Now that you have some background with the components of a spreadsheet, it is time to enter each data type and create a worksheet. As mentioned, entering data always begins by designating the current cell. This is done by using the arrow keys or by using the mouse pointer and clicking on a desired cell. The next step is to enter the data.

With ClarisWorks, the first character entered automatically determines the type of data. For example, when a letter is typed first, ClarisWorks automatically assumes the entry of a label. When a number is typed first, ClarisWorks assumes a value. While this works most of the time, there are exceptions. You have already seen that a formula or a function must begin with the equal sign. Without the equal sign, for example, ClarisWorks would see SUM as a label and would not use it to calculate.

As you enter data into the cell, the data does not appear within the cell. Instead, it appears along the top of the screen in the entry bar. This bar contains the current cell address; an X, which is the Accept button; a check mark, which is the Cancel button; and the contents of the cell. Only when you press the Return key or move the current cell indicator will the results of the data entry appear within the cell. As a general rule, you must complete data entry into a cell by pressing Return. Once data is in a cell, each time you move the current cell indicator onto the cell, the contents of the cell will appear in the entry bar.

Hands-On

1. Start ClarisWorks.

2. From the New Document dialog box, select Spreadsheet.

   The spreadsheet document looks very different from the word processing document. In addition, notice the (SS) in the title bar of this window, marking this as a spreadsheet document. Your screen should be similar to Figure 4-3.

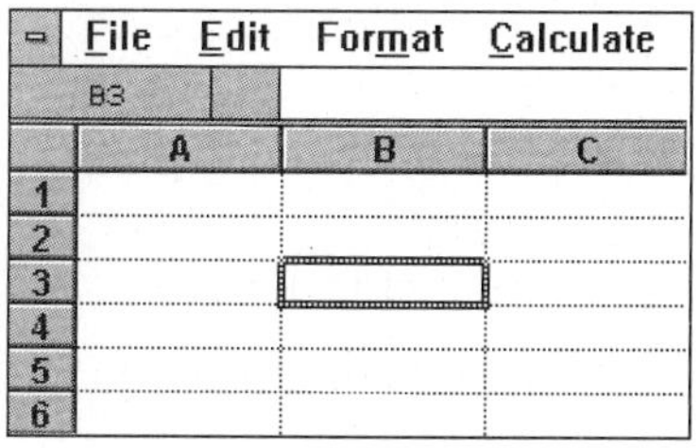

3. Move the mouse pointer to cell B3 and click.

   The current cell indicator appears, as shown in Figure 4-4.

4. Use the arrow keys to activate cell B2.

5. Type **Income** in cell B2.

   As you type Income, it appears in the entry bar, not in the current cell. If you make a mistake, press (Enter) , move the current cell indicator back to cell B2, and type again.

6. Press (Enter) and notice that cell B2 contains the label Income. The current cell indicator automatically moves to cell B3.

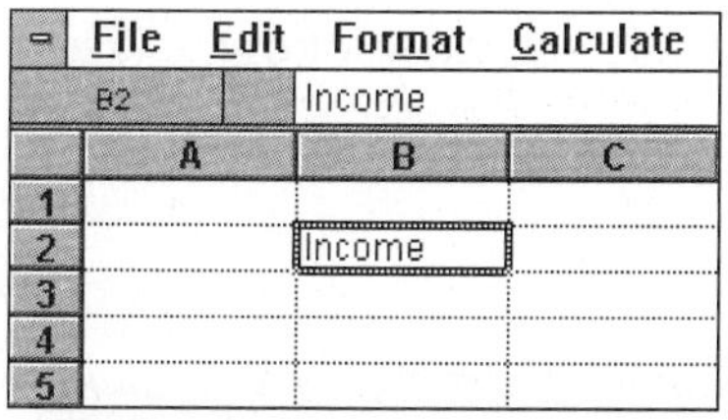

7. Move the current cell indicator to cell B2.

   The contents of B2 appear in the entry bar as well as in the cell. See Figure 4-5.

8. Type the following, shown in Figure 4-6.

B3 **Wages and Tips**	B4 **Second Income**
B5 **Alimony**	B6 **Loans**
B7 **Total Income**	B9 **Expense**
B10 **Mortgage**	B11 **Auto**
B12 **Utilities**	B13 **Entertainment**
B14 **Tuition**	B15 **Total Expense**
B17 **Balance**	

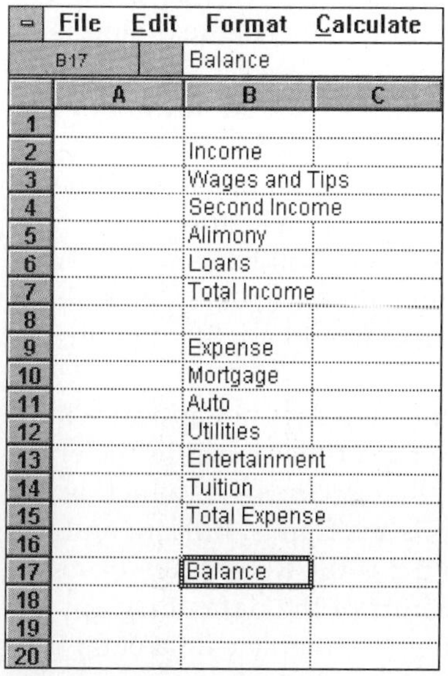

9. In column C, type the following values. See Figure 4-7.

   Notice that no values are added next to any of the totals, nor the balance.

C3 (Wages and Tips) **225**	C4 (Second Income) **50**
C5 (Alimony) **100**	C6 (Loans) **125**
C7 (Total Income)	C9 (Expense)
C10 (Mortgage) **500**	C11 (Auto) **350**
C12 (Utilities) **75**	C13 (Entertainment) **50**
C14 (Tuition) **250**	C15 (Total Expense)
C17 (Balance)	

FIGURE 4-4

FIGURE 4-5

FIGURE 4-6

⊟	File	Edit	Format	Calculate	Options

C14	250

	A	B	C	D
1				
2		Income		
3		Wages and ⌐	225	
4		Second Inco	50	
5		Alimony	100	
6		Loans	125	
7		Total Income		
8				
9		Expense		
10		Mortgage	500	
11		Auto	350	
12		Utilities	75	
13		Entertainmei	50	
14		Tuition	250	
15		Total Expense		
16				
17		Balance		
18				
19				
20				

FIGURE 4-7

10. Now it's time to add some formulas. In cell C7 (next to Total Income) enter the following formula: **=C3+C4+C5+C6**. In cell C15 (next to Total Expense) enter: **=C10+C11+C12+C13+C14**. In cell C17, type the formula to calculate a balance: **=C7-C15**.

Only the results of the formula appear in the cell. The formula appears in the entry bar, as shown in Figure 4-8.

11. The balance for this budget is unfortunately a negative number (-725). Since you are not the government, something must be done. Increase your wages to 1,000 and notice the effect on both the total income and the balance.

12. Move the current cell indicator to C7, across from Total Income.

13. Type the following function: **=SUM(C3..C6)** and press ⌐Enter⌐.

The contents of the cell in the entry bar reflect the new function, yet the result is the same. See Figure 4-9.

14. Change the formula in cell C15 (across from Total Expense) to a function that will produce the same result as the current formula.

FIGURE 4-8

⊟	File	Edit	Format	Calculate	Options	Window	Help		⬍

C17	=C7-C15

	A	B	C	D	E	F	G	H	⬆
1									
2		Income							
3		Wages and ⌐	225						
4		Second Inco	50						
5		Alimony	100						
6		Loans	125						
7		Total Income	500						
8									
9		Expense							
10		Mortgage	500						
11		Auto	350						
12		Utilities	75						
13		Entertainmei	50						
14		Tuition	250						
15		Total Expens	1225						
16									
17		Balance	-725						
18									
19									

FIGURE 4-9

⊟	File	Edit	Format	Calculate	Options	Window	Help		⬍

C7	=SUM(C3..C6)

	A	B	C	D	E	F	G	H	⬆
1									
2		Income							
3		Wages and ⌐	1000						
4		Second Inco	50						
5		Alimony	100						
6		Loans	125						
7		Total Income	1275						
8									
9		Expense							
10		Mortgage	500						
11		Auto	350						
12		Utilities	75						
13		Entertainmei	50						
14		Tuition	250						
15		Total Expens	1225						
16									
17		Balance	50						
18									
19									

Exercise 4-1   Take a few minutes to change any of the values for income and expense items. Notice how these changes affect the totals and the balance. Now, adjust both income and expense items to reach a zero balance.

SAVING A WORKSHEET

With ClarisWorks, saving a spreadsheet document is done in the same way as saving a word processing document. You should use the Save As command the first time you save a document and specify the drive, directory, and file name. Once saved, you may update or resave the document at any time by simply choosing the Save option from the File menu.

1. Save your first worksheet on your disk as FIRSTWS.CWK.

    Be sure you select your disk, not the hard disk, as the location to save the document file. Notice the new name of the worksheet appears in the title bar.

EDITING A WORKSHEET

Editing the contents of a cell is similar to editing a document on a word processor. While typing a cell entry, but before pressing the Enter key, it is possible to use the delete key to delete characters. Once data is in a cell, however, you have two basic options. First, you can replace the contents of a cell by simply retyping. You can also edit the contents of a cell by placing the pointer in the entry bar, then clicking to activate the insertion point. Once the insertion point is active, you can make any changes you want to the cell contents.

If you inadvertently add data to a cell and you want to erase the contents of the cell, you must follow two simple steps. First, move the current cell indicator to the desired cell, then select Clear from the Edit menu. Clear erases the contents of the cell but does not remove the cell from the worksheet. You may also press the Del or Delete key to erase the current cell.

1. Activate cell A1.

2. Type the following: **Personal Financial Statement** [Enter]

    Notice the contents of cell A1 cannot fit in the width of cell A1. For now, don't worry about this.

3. Move back to cell A1 and click the pointer at the end of the entry bar. This causes the insertion point to appear at the end of the label.

4. Add your name and press ⌅Enter .

    See Figure 4-10. Notice the modification to the contents
    of the cell.

FIGURE 4-10

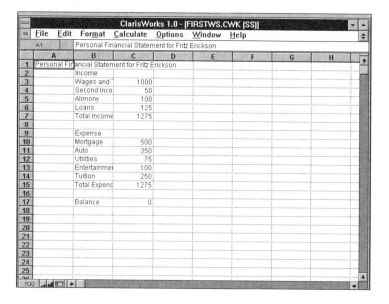

Inserting and Deleting Cells

It is also possible to insert or delete rows and columns by using the
Insert Cells and Delete Cells options in the Calculate menu. To insert
one row of cells, you must first select where the new row of cells
will appear. This is done by clicking on the desired cell address. You
may insert more than one row or column by clicking and dragging
to select as many rows or columns as you desire. Deleting rows and
columns also requires that you select one or more rows or columns.

When you insert or delete rows and columns, any formulas
will automatically adjust to these changes in the worksheet. For example, if you insert a row that will reside in the middle of a function
or formula, the function or formula will automatically add the row.
If you delete a row that is referenced in a function or formula, again,
ClarisWorks will automatically make the necessary adjustments.

Hands-On

1. Move the mouse pointer to row 2 and click.

    This selects all the cells in row 2.

2. Select Insert Cells from the Calculate menu.

    A new row of cells is inserted in the worksheet as shown
    in Figure 4-11.

FIGURE 4-11

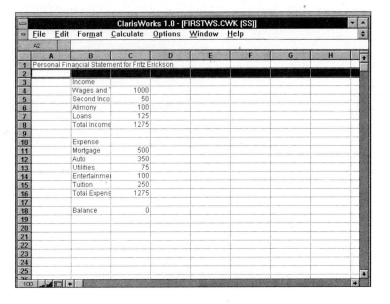

3. Go to cell C8 and notice the range of cells within the function changed to C4..C7 to accommodate the insertion of the new row.

4. Insert two new rows at row 9.

5. Select the two new rows you just added and choose the Delete Cells option in the Calculate menu.

This inserts, then deletes, two rows of cells.

Copying Cells

On many occasions, the same formulas or functions may be re-used with only slight modifications. For example, with a grade sheet, the teacher may want to average a row of cells for each student. The same formula may be re-used with only slight modifications to the cell addresses for each student. Rather than re-type each formula, it is quicker and easier to copy the formula in a cell and make the alterations to each formula as it is copied.

ClarisWorks makes it easy to copy data from a cell (or a group of cells) to another cell (or group of cells) and alter the formulas or functions for each row or column. For example, it's easy to copy a formula written for one student's grades for each additional student in the class.

The first step in copying is to select a range of cells to copy. This can include an entire row or column, or a block of cells within a row or column. To select specific cells, simply move the mouse pointer to the beginning of the desired range, then click and drag to the end of the range. This is virtually the same process used with word processing. Once a block is selected, the next step is to select either Cut or Copy from the Edit menu. Cut removes the original; copy leaves the original block on the worksheet.

Once a range is selected, the next step is to choose the location to copy to. This is done by clicking the mouse pointer at the beginning cell, rather than blocking the entire new location. The last step is to select the Paste option from the Edit menu. If only one cell is copied, you may paste the one cell to a block of cells. This is often the case if you create one formula and you wish to use the same formula in several rows or columns.

Hands-On

1. Move the mouse pointer to cell C4, across from Wages.

2. Click, hold, and drag to cell C18. Release the mouse button. This selects the block of cells as shown in Figure 4-12.

3. Select the Copy option from the Edit menu.

4. Move the mouse pointer and click on cell D4.

5. Select the Paste option from the Edit menu.

   All cells are copied to column D.

6. Move the current cell indicator to D8.

   Notice the function in D8 represents the data for column D, even though it was copied from column C. See Figure 4-13.

7. At cell C2, type **January** and at D2, type **February**

8. In column E, add data for March.

FIGURE 4-12

		ClarisWorks 1.0 - [FIRSTWS.CWK [SS]]						
File	Edit	Format	Calculate	Options	Window	Help		
C4		1000						
	A	B	C	D	E	F	G	H
1	Personal Financial Statement for Fritz Erickson							
2								
3		Income						
4		Wages and	1000					
5		Second Inco	50					
6		Alimony	100					
7		Loans	125					
8		Total Income	1275					
9								
10		Expense						
11		Mortgage	500					
12		Auto	350					
13		Utilities	75					
14		Entertainme	100					
15		Tuition	250					
16		Total Expens	1275					
17								
18		Balance	0					
19								
20								
21								
22								
23								
24								
25								

100

FIGURE 4-13

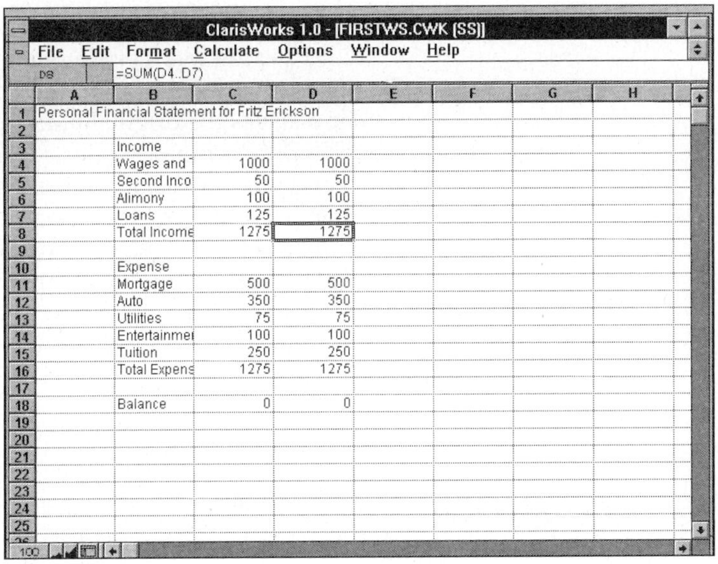

ClarisWorks 1.0 - [FIRSTWS.CWK (SS)]

	A	B	C	D	E	F	G	H
1	Personal Financial Statement for Fritz Erickson							
2								
3		Income						
4		Wages and	1000	1000				
5		Second Inco	50	50				
6		Alimony	100	100				
7		Loans	125	125				
8		Total Income	1275	1275				
9								
10		Expense						
11		Mortgage	500	500				
12		Auto	350	350				
13		Utilities	75	75				
14		Entertainme	100	100				
15		Tuition	250	250				
16		Total Expens	1275	1275				
17								
18		Balance	0	0				
19								
20								

D8 =SUM(D4..D7)

Exercise 4-2   Now that you have data for three months, change the values for each income and expense item. Changes made for one column affect only that column. Be sure that the balance for each month remains at zero.

Absolute and Relative Cell Addresses

When copying formulas or inserting or deleting columns and rows, it is important to consider the issue of absolute versus relative cell addresses. Copying a formula using an absolute cell address causes the formula to remain the same in both cells. In other words, absolute addresses make exact copies and do not change the calculation to fit a new location. For example, copying the function =SUM(A1..A5) from cell A6 to cell B6 results in cell B6 displaying the sum of cells A1 to A5. This can pose a problem if you wanted the sum of cells B1 to B5. Using a relative address causes the function to change to fit the new column.

Fortunately, ClarisWorks always uses a relative address unless you specify absolute addresses. To specify an absolute address, you must place a dollar sign ($) before the cell and row address. For example, =SUM(A1..A5) uses a relative reference. The function =SUM(A1..A5) is an absolute address. Notice that the dollar sign ($) must be in front of each component of the address (row *and* column).

Recalculating

Worksheets can get very large. They can have hundreds of formulas and functions. Each time new data are added to the worksheet, ClarisWorks recalculates. For extremely large worksheets, recalculating all the formulas and functions for each new piece of data can interrupt the user and become somewhat annoying.

ClarisWorks provides two calculation options. The first is Auto Calc. With this option selected, every change in the spreadsheet will result in a complete recalculation. If you do not want to use this feature, you may select Auto Calc to remove the check mark. Removing the check mark disables this feature. Once it is disabled, use the Calculate Now option to recalculate the worksheet on demand. If your worksheet becomes excessively slow, you may want to disable Auto Calc and use Calculate Now. As long as everything is working fine, it is a good idea to use Auto Calc.

Order of Operations

When using formulas with multiple processes, it is important to consider the order of operations—the order in which mathematical processes are performed. The following lists this order.

( ) any operation within parentheses has precedence over all other operations

% percentage (divides a number by 100)

^ exponentiation

*, / multiplication and division

+, - addition and subtraction

If two operations are at the same level, the order of operations is from left to right.

The formula =A1+B1/C1 will produce a different outcome than will =(A1+B1)/C1. In the first case, B1/C1 is done first, followed by the addition of A1. In the second case, A1 will be added to B1, with the results being divided by C1.

More on Functions

ClarisWorks makes it easy to add functions by using the Paste Function option in the Edit Menu. This option produces a list of functions; you may choose one to paste into a cell. Once pasted, all that is needed is to replace the variable with a specific cell address. For example, instead of typing =SUM(A1..A5), you could select the SUM function from the Paste Function option, then select the desired cell range.

Whether you type a function or select it from the Paste Function option, it is possible to designate the range by mouse, rather than typing the range from the keyboard. By clicking and dragging on a range of cells as you create a formula or function, that range is then defined within the formula or function. This takes a bit of practice, but once you become accomplished, entering formulas and functions becomes very easy.

Hands-On

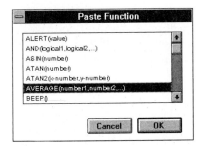

FIGURE 4-14

FIGURE 4-15

FIGURE 4-16

1. Move the current cell indicator to cell F4 (across from Wages and Tips).

2. Select Paste Function from the Edit menu.

3. Use the scroll bar to locate AVERAGE. See Figure 4-14.

4. Click on AVERAGE, then click on OK.

   This function is added to your worksheet at the location of the current cell. See Figure 4-15.

5. In the data entry bar, delete *number1,number 2,..*

6. Place the mouse pointer on cell C4, click, hold, and drag to cell E4.

   Notice that the range is added to the function.

7. Press Enter .

8. Copy this function to produce an average for all items in your worksheet. See Figure 4-16.

FORMATTING

The values in a budget worksheet are normally expressed in dollars and cents, but it is not necessary to type in dollar signs. ClarisWorks allows you to format numbers in a variety of ways. You can choose whether or not to display dollar signs, where to place commas, and can control the number of decimal places. These data formats can vary from cell to cell or be set for an entire worksheet.

The process of determining the numeric format begins by selecting the cell or cells to include in the format, done by blocking them. Once you select a group of cells, the next step is to select Number from the Format menu, which produces a variety of Number options. You may select any combination you desire. It is also possible to select a group of cells and set the Date and Time format as desired, using the same process.

In addition to adjusting number formats, it is possible to specify type fonts, styles, and sizes for both numeric and label data. Using these options helps create visually appealing worksheets. The process of setting Fonts, Size, Style, and Text Color are virtually the same as with word processing; first select the cell or range of cells, then select the desired attribute. However, as with word processing, use care when emphasizing data with these options. Overuse of typographical emphasis can distract and confuse the reader.

The alignment of data in columns and rows can also be adjusted for both numeric and label data. Data can be aligned at the left edge, right edge, or center of the cell. Numeric data can be aligned along decimal points as well. Again, just select the cell or cells, then assign the desired alignment attribute.

Hands-On

1. Activate cell A1.

2. Select Helvetica from Font in the Format menu.

3. For cell A1, select 14 point from Size in the Format menu.

4. For cell A1, select Bold from Style in the Format menu. See Figure 4-17.

5. Select cells C4 through C18.

6. From the Format menu, choose Number.

   This produces the Numeric dialog box.

7. Click on the button next to Currency, and make sure Precision is set to 2. See Figure 4-18.

8. Click on OK and notice the resulting change, shown in Figure 4-19.

   Notice the Precision setting sets the Currency to two decimal places.

FIGURE 4-17

	ClarisWorks 1.0 - [FIRSTWS.CWK [SS]]						
File Edit Format Calculate Options Window Help							
A1	Personal Financial Statement for Fritz Erickson						

	A	B	C	D	E	F	G	H
1	Personal Financial Statement for Fritz Erickson							
2			January	February	March			
3		Income						
4		Wages and	1000	2000	3000	2000		
5		Second Inco	50	50	50	50		
6		Alimony	100	100	100	100		
7		Loans	125	125	125	125		
8		Total Income	1275	2275	3275	2275		
9								
10		Expense						
11		Mortgage	500	500	500	500		
12		Auto	350	350	350	350		
13		Utilities	75	75	75	75		
14		Entertainme	100	100	100	100		
15		Tuition	250	250	250	250		
16		Total Expens	1275	1275	1275	1275		
17								
18		Balance	0	1000	2000	1000		
19								
20								
21								
22								
23								
24								
25								

100

FIGURE 4-18

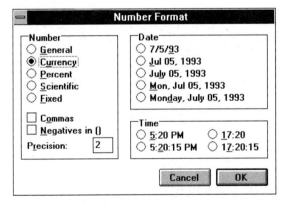

Number Format

Number
- ○ General
- ● Currency
- ○ Percent
- ○ Scientific
- ○ Fixed

- ☐ Commas
- ☐ Negatives in ()

Precision: 2

Date
- ○ 7/5/93
- ○ Jul 05, 1993
- ○ July 05, 1993
- ○ Mon, Jul 05, 1993
- ○ Monday, July 05, 1993

Time
- ○ 5:20 PM   ○ 17:20
- ○ 5:20:15 PM   ○ 17:20:15

Cancel   OK

FIGURE 4-19

	ClarisWorks 1.0 - [FIRSTWS.CWK [SS]]						
File Edit Format Calculate Options Window Help							
C4	1000						

	A	B	C	D	E	F	G	H
1	Personal Financial Statement for Fritz Erickson							
2			January	February	March			
3		Income						
4		Wages and	$1000.00	2000	3000	2000		
5		Second Inco	$50.00	50	50	50		
6		Alimony	$100.00	100	100	100		
7		Loans	$125.00	125	125	125		
8		Total Income	$1275.00	2275	3275	2275		
9								
10		Expense						
11		Mortgage	$500.00	500	500	500		
12		Auto	$350.00	350	350	350		
13		Utilities	$75.00	75	75	75		
14		Entertainme	$100.00	100	100	100		
15		Tuition	$250.00	250	250	250		
16		Total Expens	$1275.00	1275	1275	1275		
17								
18		Balance	$0.00	1000	2000	1000		
19								
20								
21								
22								
23								
24								
25								

100

9. With cells C4 through C18 selected, set the alignment to Center with the Alignment option in the Format menu.

Notice that the numbers in the specified cells align within the center of each cell, as shown in Figure 4-20.

FIGURE 4-20

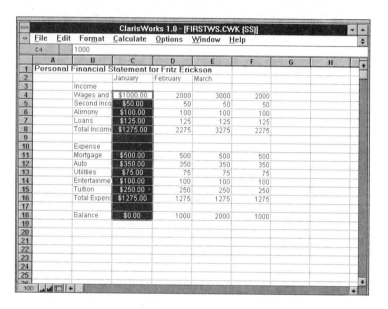

Exercise 4-4 Now that you have had a chance to use some of the formatting capabilities of the ClarisWorks spreadsheet, it's time to practice. Take a few minutes to make your spreadsheet as attractive as possible. Use your own ideas to determine the font, style, and size of both labels and values, and alignment.

Setting Column Width

One of the most important formatting features of ClarisWorks is the ability to adjust the width of one or more columns. Whenever labels in a cell are wider than the current cell width, the label spills over to the next cells. Even though the label resides in its original cell, it *appears* to reside in multiple cells. The problem of values that are wider than cells is even more severe. Any time a value is wider than a cell, the entire value appears as a series of pound signs (#).

The easiest way to adjust a single column is to place the mouse pointer on the left edge of the column, next to the column letter. This changes the cursor to a two-way arrow. To adjust the width of the cell, simply click and drag to the left or right.

For more precision, it is a good idea to activate the ruler by selecting Show Rulers from the Window menu. With the rulers displayed, you can set column widths very precisely.

Hands-On

1. Select Show Rulers from the Window menu.

   Notice that each column is one inch wide.

2. Place the mouse pointer on the line dividing columns B and C. This produces a two-way arrow.

3. Click and drag this line to the right to expand the width of column B to one and one half inches. See Figure 4-21.

4. Adjust the width of any other column to improve the appearance of your worksheet.

FIGURE 4-21

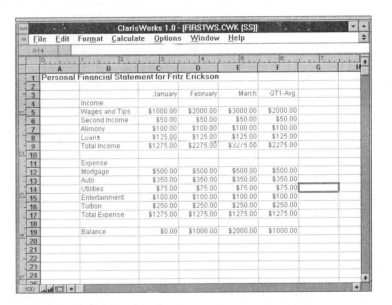

PRINTING

Printing a worksheet is not much different from printing a word processing document. However, there are a few important considerations. When printing, you may print the entire document or print a selected range of cells. To print the entire document, just select Print from the File menu. To print a range of cells, first block the cells you want to print, then select the Print option from the File menu.

If the worksheet you print does not appear as you desire, there are several choices. Using the Document option in the Format menu, you may set the margins and set the size of the document. With Size, you may set the number of rows and columns to be included within your worksheet.

Spreadsheets are usually wider than they are long. However, if you print on a standard 8.5 by 11 inch sheet, the paper is longer than it is wide. You may change this by changing the orientation of the printed page. When a page appears longer than it is wide, it is known as a *portrait* orientation. If you turn the page on its side, it is a *landscape* orientation. To change the orientation, you must use the Print Setup option in the File menu. This produces the Print Setup dialog box for the printer you are using. At the bottom of this dialog box is the orientation setting. Here, you may choose portrait or landscape.

Never try to print a worksheet before saving. Printing is one of the major sources of problems with all applications software. If the printer fails during the printing of a worksheet, and before saving, the entire worksheet and several hours of work can easily be wasted. *Always* save the worksheet file on a disk before issuing a print command.

1. Save your worksheet on disk.
2. Select Print Setup from the File menu.

   Notice the Print Setup dialog box for your printer. See Figure 4-22.

3. Set the orientation to landscape.
4. Click on OK.
5. Select Print from the File menu.

   This produces the same Print dialog box used for word processing.

6. Click on OK to print your document.

FIGURE 4-22

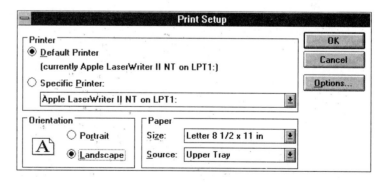

Exercise 4-5   Now that you have printed your document, use the options in the Document box from the Format menu to make any adjustments needed. Do whatever you feel is necessary to improve the presentation of your document on paper.

USING CHARTS

While worksheets can provide a lot of information, it is easy to get lost in numbers and difficult to get an overall view of the data. Too much information may cause confusion. For this reason, the spreadsheet within ClarisWorks offers the ability to represent numeric data in charts.

With ClarisWorks, you can create seven different types of charts from spreadsheet data. These are the Bar, Stacked Bar, Line, Scatter, Pie, and X-Y charts. Even if you don't know what all these charts look like, ClarisWorks makes it easy to create any of these types of charts.

Every chart begins by selecting a range of cells to chart the worksheet. This can be a set of values and labels in rows and columns. This data will be depicted by the chart. For example, the bars in a bar chart represent the selected range of cells.

Once a cell range is identified, the next step is to select the Make Chart option from the Options menu. This produces a dialog box containing the categories of available charts and chart options. All you have to do is select the category and options you want, then click on OK.

The chart options depend on which type of chart you intend to create. One of the more popular chart options is the Legend. Legends contain names or other forms of data identification. This helps define each item within a chart.

Once you create a chart, it appears in the worksheet. It is possible to move the chart anywhere within the worksheet or place it in the clipboard for access by the word processor or other ClarisWorks applications by using the chart handles.

Hands-On

1. Select cells B5 through C8, the income items for the month of January. See Figure 4-23.

2. Select Make Chart from the Options menu.

   This produces the Make Chart dialog box.

FIGURE 4-23

	ClarisWorks 1.0 - [FIRSTWS.CWK [SS]]						
File	Edit	Format	Calculate	Options	Window	Help	
B5	Wages and Tips						
	A	B	C	D	E	F	G	H
1	Personal Financial Statement for Fritz Erickson						
2							
3			January	February	March	QT1-Avg.	
4		Income					
5		Wages and Tips	$1000.00	$2000.00	$3000.00	$2000.00	
6		Second Income	$50.00	$50.00	$50.00	$50.00	
7		Alimony	$100.00	$100.00	$100.00	$100.00	
8		Loans	$125.00	$125.00	$125.00	$125.00	
9		Total Income	$1275.00	$2275.00	$3275.00	$2275.00	
10							
11		Expense					
12		Mortgage	$500.00	$500.00	$500.00	$500.00	
13		Auto	$350.00	$350.00	$350.00	$350.00	
14		Utilities	$75.00	$75.00	$75.00	$75.00	
15		Entertainment	$100.00	$100.00	$100.00	$100.00	
16		Tuition	$250.00	$250.00	$250.00	$250.00	
17		Total Expense	$1275.00	$1275.00	$1275.00	$1275.00	
18							
19		Balance	$0.00	$1000.00	$2000.00	$1000.00	
20							
21							
22							
23							
24							

3.   Click on Pie under Categories.

4.   Click on OK and notice the pie chart, shown in Figure 4-24.

5.   Click anywhere in the chart and drag it to the left.

     You can put the chart anywhere within your worksheet.

6.   From the Options menu, select Modify Chart.

     The Make Chart dialog box reappears.

7.   Click on Bar, then on OK.

     Notice this converts the chart to a Bar Chart. See Figure 4-25.

8.   Select Modify Chart, then select Stacked Bar.

9.   Click on OK.

     A stacked bar chart appears, shown in Figure 4-26.

FIGURE 4-24

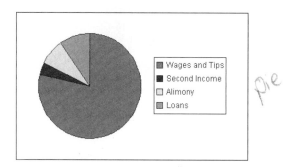

FIGURE 4-25

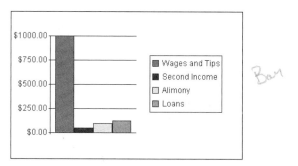

FIGURE 4-26

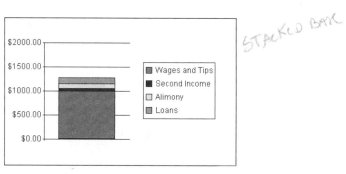

Chart Types

How you design a chart, and the chart options you select, are influenced in large part by the type of chart you intend to create. ClarisWorks will chart any data you want. However, it is up to you to determine which data are meaningful. To give you an idea of what each chart is able to do, the following is a brief description of each chart type.

Bar   A bar chart displays data in colors or patterns with each color or pattern representing a data series. You may create horizontal or vertical charts. Bar charts are among the most useful for comparing values. See Figure 4-27.

FIGURE 4-27

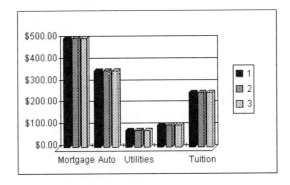

Stacked bar   Stacked bars display cumulative data. For example, data within a division are displayed within the same bar. Like bar charts, stacked bar charts are popular for comparing data in one column or row to another column or row. See Figure 4-28.

FIGURE 4-28

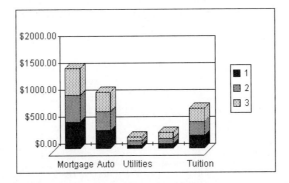

Line   One of the most popular charts is the line chart. This type of chart displays data as a series of points, each point connected by a line. Line charts are often used to track data as it changes over time. For example, sales forecasts are often depicted with line charts. Figure 4-29 shows a line chart.

FIGURE 4-29

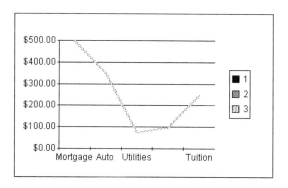

X-Y X-Y line charts plot data on X-Y axis coordinates, then connect the points with a line. Two columns of data must be used, with each row representing both X and Y locations. This type of chart is useful for many types of statistical data. See Figure 4-30.

FIGURE 4-30

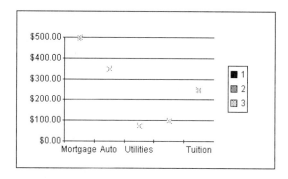

Scatter Scatter charts plot data at points within a chart. This is like a line chart without the line. Like line charts, scatter charts are good for examining how data changes over time. See Figure 4-31.

FIGURE 4-31

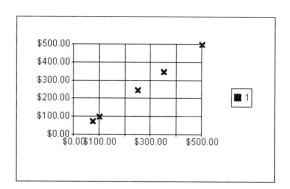

Pie Pie charts compare data as a percentage or portion of a whole. Typically, pie charts are limited to related types of data. With Claris-Works, you may have a standard pie chart or an exploding pie. Figure 4-32 shows a standard pie chart.

FIGURE 4-32

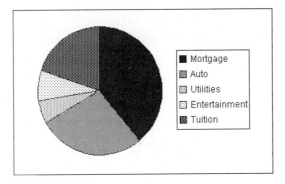

Exercise 4-6 Working with charts requires a great deal of practice and a bit of patience. Use the data in the sample worksheet and see how many different, meaningful types of charts you can create. The important word here is *meaningful*—charts that are nice to look at but have little or no meaning should be discarded. Also, experiment with the different options to improve the overall appearance of each chart. Be sure to print each chart.

Summary

- A spreadsheet is applications software designed to support mathematical calculations on organized numerical information.

- In spreadsheets, worksheets organize information. *into a grid of cells*

- A worksheet is a grid of cells. *th. Contain words.*

- Cells can contain words (to serve as labels), numbers, or formulas (to perform calculations.)

- Worksheet cells are organized in columns and rows. Columns are generally identified by letter and rows by number.

- A cell name refers to one single cell (for example, B3).

- Several cells in sequence are called a *range*.

- There are four basic types of data—labels, values, date/time, and formulas.

- Labels are text entries that describe the numeric content of other cells.

- Labels may contain numbers, but labels cannot be any part of a mathematical operation.

- Values are numbers that are available for manipulation.

- Formulas are the means for mathematically manipulating the values in cells.

- Date/time data allow you to enter dates and times that can be serially compared.
- The strength of a spreadsheet is in its use of formulas and functions.
- Before entering data, be sure to move the current cell indicator.
- When a letter is typed first, ClarisWorks assumes the entry of a label.
- It is possible to insert or delete rows and columns by using the Insert Cells and Delete Cells options in the Calculate menu.
- If your worksheet becomes excessively slow, you may want to disable Auto Calc and use Calculate Now.
- Never print a worksheet before saving.

Questions

1. Spreadsheets require information to be entered in _____cell_____ locations.
2. Cells are organized into _____columns_____ and _____rows_____ .
3. A reference to a sequence of several cells that identifies the first and last cell in the sequence is called a _____range_____ .
4. There are four types of spreadsheet data: _____labels_____ , _____values_____ , _____day time_____ , and _____formulas_____ .
5. _____labels_____ are never manipulated mathematically.
6. The real strength of a spreadsheet is its use of _____formulas_____ and _____functions_____ .
7. _____stacked bar____ charts are most useful for displaying cumulative data.
8. Once you create a chart, the chart appears within the _____worksheet_____ .
9. Every chart must be based on a _____worksheet / range of cells, based on____
10. It is possible to change an existing chart by using the _____modify chart_____ option.

Quiz

1. What is the first step for placing data in a cell?
   a. use the function option instead of a formula
   b. move the current cell indicator to the desired cell
   c. press the Enter key
   d. press the equal sign

2. Cell width is a spreadsheet constant and cannot be changed.
   a. true
   b. false

3. Which type of data does not allow for mathematical operations?
   a. value
   b. formula
   c. label
   d. function

4. Cells are organized into:
   a. columns and rows
   b. formulas and functions
   c. memory allocation variables
   d. random linear arrangements

5. What do two dots (..) indicate in a spreadsheet?
   a. a cell
   b. a range of cells
   c. a function
   d. a formula

6. Which of the following is best suited for adding the contents of 200 cells?
   a. value
   b. formula
   c. label
   d. function

7. Charts generated by the spreadsheet program can be used only within the spreadsheet.
   a. true
   b. false

8. Which type of data automatically aligns along the right edge of a cell?
   a. label
   b. value
   c. formula
   d. function

9. Which of the following is most useful for averaging the contents of 200 cells?
   a. label
   b. value
   c. formula
   d. function

10. Which type of chart is appropriate for comparing data over time?
    a. line
    b. X-Y
    c. pie
    d. all are appropriate

Applications

1. By hand, draw out a spreadsheet to calculate grades for a class. In one column, list all the required assignments. In

another column, make up grades already earned and leave space for grades that have not been completed. At the bottom, write down the calculation procedures needed to calculate the final grade.

2. Maintaining sports statistics can be a time-consuming process. Pick any sport and develop an outline for a spreadsheet to maintain the appropriate statistics. For example, what columns and rows are needed to keep statistics on the batting averages of baseball players, handicap scores of golfers, times for swimmers, or scores for gymnasts?

3. Create your own worksheet to calculate your college expenses and income (or other resources). Be sure to note the types of calculations needed and the locations of these calculations. In addition, create a line for totals. Does your income equal your payments? If not, what changes could you make to balance income and expenses?

5

DATABASE ESSENTIALS

OBJECTIVES

Learning the material in this chapter will enable you to:

- describe a database
- identify the primary components of a ClarisWorks database
- distinguish among data file, record, and field
- use a variety of layouts with one data file
- create useable fields
- describe the different types of fields
- plan a data file
- add data to fields
- delete records from a data file
- search for data contained within selected records
- sort records
- generate reports
- use the Mail Merge feature of word processing

OVERVIEW

Maintaining records has always been a major problem. Just consider what it takes to keep track of student grades at your school. Not only do instructors have to maintain records of student grades, but the school must keep grades on file to produce transcripts, generate grade point averages, and a host of other activities. Before files became computerized, every student had a paper file where all grades were stored. At the end of each semester, someone had to locate and pull each file from large sets of file cabinets. The next step involved writing entries into specific locations within the file—a place for each course grade, a place for attendance, a place for disciplinary data, and so on. The last step was to return the file to its proper location in the file cabinet and hope the data entry, as well as the filing, were accurate. If you had 25,000 students, this was a major task. If you had 250 students, it was still a big task.

Manual data collection and examination wastes time and is prone to a high degree of error. It is laborious to add files to the file cabinets and add data to individual paper files. It also takes a great deal of time to pull pieces of information from selected records. Imagine what it must have taken to calculate the average GPA for math majors.

Today, rather than searching through piles of paper to locate a file or to find specific data in several files, database software performs these tasks very efficiently. Instead of storing data in paper files, database software stores data electronically on a disk. Instead of requiring an army of people to search through a file cabinet for one bit of information from many files, database software makes it easy to search through all files almost instantaneously.

This chapter provides the basic knowledge needed to begin to use the database portion of ClarisWorks for storing and retrieving data. As with the previous two chapters, you will need to practice many of the skills discussed in this chapter. Only after practicing can you use this database software effectively.

DATABASE ESSENTIALS

In its simplest form, database software makes it possible for computers to store and retrieve large sets of data. In some ways, all computer applications are types of database software. Certainly, a word processor stores documents as data and a spreadsheet stores worksheets as data. But neither of these types of programs is database software.

For software to be considered database software, it must provide users with a quick and easy means of storing, recalling, sorting, and reporting on a wide range of data. Unlike the ClarisWorks word processor, which only stores text, or the spreadsheet, which primarily stores numbers, the database stores almost any type of data. This can include grades, address lists, extracurricular activities, or student medical information. The strength of database software is its ability to recall data quickly and efficiently. With a word processor, you cannot search for a group of addresses within the same document. With a database, you can.

The ClarisWorks database contains two primary components— a data file and a series of layouts. A *data file* is a document containing all data within the database. This data resides in the document in a highly structured and organized fashion. For example, a data file may contain the names, addresses, phone numbers, and grades of all students in a school. A data file may store data for a check entry system. Also, data entry screens permit unique presentations, such as shown in Figure 5-1.

A *layout* is the mechanism for examining and manipulating the data file. The layout determines how to add, edit, delete, and view data. For example, you may have one layout for entering student grades. You may have another layout for generating a mailing list. If you want to examine only students who have passed an algebra class, it is the layout that displays selected data from the data file.

FIGURE 5-1

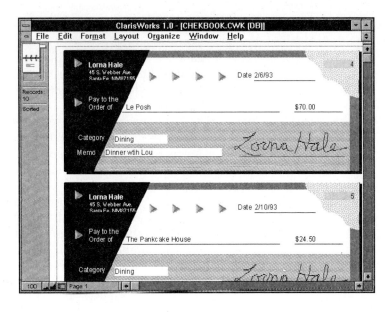

Data Files

Every data file is made up of two critical components—records and fields. *Records* are collections of data related to a single entity, such as a person or a place. For example, a data file of student records normally contains a record for each student. All records in a file have discrete names for identification.

Just as data files are made up of records, records are made up of fields. A *field* is a specific location for the entry and storage of one set of data, identified by a field name. For student records, each record normally contains several fields. However, while data within fields are different from record to record, each record has the same set of named fields. For example, a student record database may have a field titled MATH GRADE. This field exists in every record within the database file. However, the actual grade (data) placed in a field varies from record to record. This arrangement, having each record use the same fields, is known as the database *structure*.

Naming is very important for data files, records, and fields because names identify groups of similar information. Unique data file names specify the collection of related records. Unique record names (often identified by numbers) specify the collection of related data stored in fields. Finally, each field within a record is named to identify the specific data.

When creating a data file with ClarisWorks, you must first specify each of the fields. This is called the field *definition*. Field definitions require two factors. First, you must specify a field name. For example, LAST NAME, FIRST NAME, ADDRESS, CITY, STATE, and ZIP are six different field names. In addition, you must specify the type of data to be contained in each field for each record. Table 5-1 shows the six different data types.

Table 5-1   Data Types

Type	Description
Text	Text fields are for any type of data that you can type from the keyboard. They are similar to spreadsheet labels in that they provide the most flexibility. In other words, you can put whatever you want in a text field. However, you cannot manipulate text fields mathematically.
Number	Number fields are for numeric data for mathematical computations. A grade might be identified as a number field, because you may want to calculate a grade point average.
Date	Date fields store date data. Date fields are used to store such things as the dates of transactions, dates of data entry, or the date when a record should be reviewed.
Time	Time fields store time data, for example, the time that data was entered in a record.
Calculation	Calculation fields contain values derived from other data within the data file. With this type of data, it is possible to create a field for GPA. The data within the field is calculated based on data in other (number) fields.
Summary	Summary fields are also based on data found with the data file. They often include totals and subtotals of data stored in number fields.

Database Planning

The temptation with any new database is to just start creating fields. However, this is a mistake. Before you begin to add field names or even select Database as a new document, you should take a few minutes to plan your database.

Planning is the most important activity for successfully creating a usable database. It involves organizing data to account for field names, field types, field size, and data use. Good planning leads to good database design and construction. Poor planning leads to a poor database. For example, using a field name titled NAME would normally contain both first and last name data. However, if you want to organize or sort the data file based on last name, a single field NAME will not allow you this option. It would be much more useful to have two different fields—LASTNAME and FIRSTNAME. This way, you could sort on the last name of each student. If one of the goals of the database is to list grade point averages for all students, then creating a field of number data called POINTS makes much more sense than creating a text field called GRADE.

It is also important to plan for all necessary fields. While it is possible to go back and add fields to the database structure, this may require you to modify the data in all existing records. It is much easier to have a complete and correct structure at the beginning so that all data can be entered once for each record.

Normally, the planning process begins by creating a column describing all the data to be included in the database. This initial list is not a list of field names, but rather is a description of the data. In a good database plan, a second column contains actual field names for each description. The more precise the field name, the easier it is to enter accurate data. A field name can be up to 63 characters long.

A third column should indicate the data type. This is an important consideration, because the data type influences access and use of the data. For example, a text field will accept any letter, number, or symbol, but it will not allow numeric calculations even if numbers are in this type of field. As a general rule, if the data is ever to be manipulated mathematically, or if a numeric expression will be the object of a data search, use a number field. Normally, we do not add or subtract zip code numbers, and it is easy to see these as text. But zip codes should be in a numeric field because it is common to use a numeric expression to search for records based on zip codes. For example, searching for zip codes less than 49050 and greater than 49000 is easy with numeric data, but not as easy with text data.

Table 5-2 shows a sample database plan.

Table 5-2   Planning a Database Structure

Description	Field Name	Type
Entry Date	DATE	Date
Title	TITLE	Text
First Name	FIRST NAME	Text
Last Name	LAST NAME	Text
Company Name	COMPANY	Text
Mailing Address 1	ADDRESS1	Text
Mailing Address 2	ADDRESS2	Text
City	CITY	Text
State	ST	Text
Zip Code	ZIP	Number
Purchase Date	PDATE	Number
Purchase Amount	AMOUNT	Number
Mailing List	MAIL	Text

Exercise 5-1 Your goal is to create an address book with the ClarisWorks database. Take a few minutes to plan a data file structure. Be sure to identify as many fields as you believe you might need.

Defining Fields

Once you have a data file plan, the next step is to actually create the data file structure. Begin this process by selecting Database from the New Document dialog box. This causes Define Fields dialog box to appear. This dialog box lists field names and types. Below this is the location for entering new field names. To create a new name, simply type the desired field name next to Name. Next, you must select any one of the six data types in the Type box. Once each type is selected, click on Create, and your field name and type will appear in the list of defined fields.

To create a second field, simply start typing a new field name and select the appropriate field type. Again, click on Create to add this new field to your data file. This process works for all field types *except* for calculation fields and summary fields. These are discussed later in this chapter.

 *Hands-On*

1. Start ClarisWorks and select Database from the New Document dialog box.

   This causes the Define Fields dialog box to appear, as shown in Figure 5-2. Since this is a new data file, you must begin by defining field names and types.

2. In the Name box, type **Last Name** then click on the button next to Text in the Type box.

3. Click on Create.

   Notice the field Last Name with the Text type appears in the list of defined fields. See Figure 5-3.

4. Type **First Name**.

   This automatically replaces Last Name in the Name box.

FIGURE 5-2

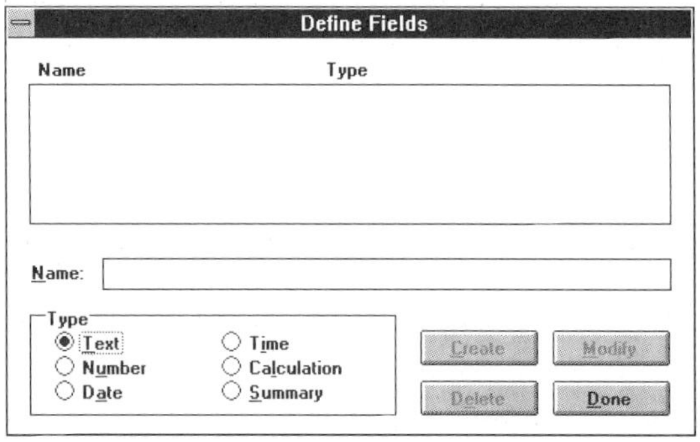

Define Fields

Name	Type

Name:

Type
- ● Text
- ○ Number
- ○ Date
- ○ Time
- ○ Calculation
- ○ Summary

Create   Modify
Delete   Done

FIGURE 5-3

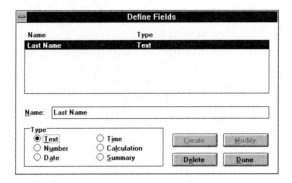

5. Select the Text type and click on Create.

   Again, notice the addition of the field to the list.

6. Add the following field definitions. See Figure 5-4.

Address	Text
City	Text
State	Text
Zip	Number
Math	Number
Science	Number
History	Number

7. Click on Done.

   Notice the data file appears on the first layout.

FIGURE 5-4

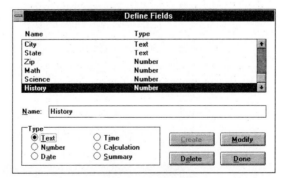

Layout 1: A Standard Layout

Every database must have both a data file and a layout. When you first create a data file, ClarisWorks automatically provides you with a layout. This default layout is called *Layout 1* (or the *standard* layout) and it appears automatically after you define the fields for the data file.

From the Layout 1 you have three basic options. First, you can use Browse to add, view, change, or sort data. It is the Browse option through which data entry occurs and where most controlling operations of the data file occur. Second, you may use the Find option to locate specific records within the data file. For example, if you want to find the record for John Smith from a data file of 1,000 records, you would use the Find option from the Layout menu. Finally, you have the option of creating a unique layout with the Layout option in the Layout menu. This option allows you to customize the way data fields are presented for both data entry and data viewing.

With Layout 1, all field names appear with text entry boxes next to each field name. It is in these boxes where all data added to a record is processed. To the left is the Book. The Book identifies which record is active, the number of records in the document, the sort status, and a bookmark.

As new records are added to the data file, each record is automatically assigned a record number. With the bookmark, you may drag this up and down to activate any record, by number, that you want.

ADDING RECORDS

After creating the field definitions, the next step is to begin adding records to the data file. This, of course, occurs through the layout. To add a record to the data file, you must select the Browse option in the Layout menu. This is the default selection after defining fields.

To enter data from Browse, simply select the text entry box next to the desired field and type. As long as you remember two simple rules, entering data is both quick and efficient. First, only data that matches the field type may be entered into each field. If you try to enter text in a number field, an error will occur. If you try to enter a name in a date field, another error will occur. In fact, ClarisWorks will not allow you to enter data of the incorrect type. The second rule comes up after typing the desired data. You may *not* press Enter to move to the next data field. Instead, you must take the mouse and click in the new field, or use the Tab key to move the insertion point to a new field. If you use the Enter key, you will expand the size of the field.

Hands-On

1. From Layout 1, place the insertion point in the box next to Last Name. Type **Cold**

2. Press the Tab key to move the insertion point to First Name. Type **Real**

3. Add the following data to each of the following fields. Refer to Figure 5-5.

Address	**123 Burr St.**
City	**Freeztail**
State	**CO**
Zip	**80113**
Math	**3**
Science	**4**
History	**3**

4. After entering all data for the first record, the next step is to enter data for the second record. To activate the second record, you must use the New Record option from the Edit menu. Select New Record and notice that the current record number changes in the Book, along with the total number of records.

5. For record 2, enter the following data, shown in Figure 5-6.

Last Name	**Hot**
First Name	**Muchto**
Address	**123 Tar St.**
City	**Sweatbox**
State	**PA**
Zip	**17551**
Math	**2**
Science	**1**
History	**3**

FIGURE 5-5

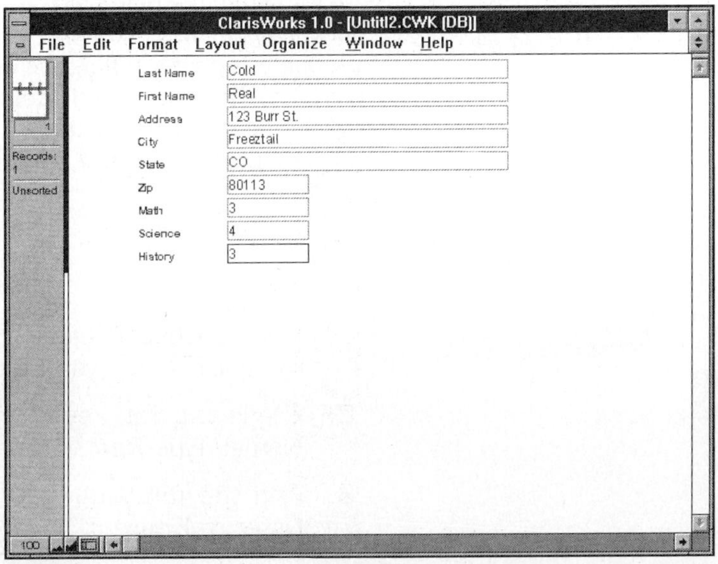

FIGURE 5-6

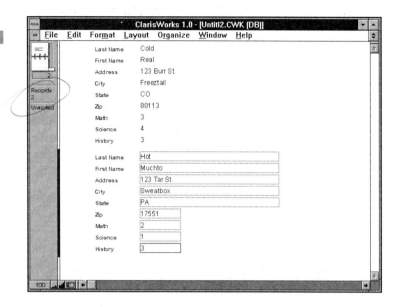

6. Add the following records to your new data file. See Figure 5-7.

Last	First	Address	City	State	Zip	Math	Sci	Hist
Foot	Big	118 Large St.	Nowhere	AK	90909	1	1	2
Pick	Nose	89 Gross St.	New York	AL	76123	4	3	4
Socks	Smelly	17 Stink St.	LaSalle	CO	80645	3	1	1
Dweb	Da	1 Smart St.	Pocket	IL	23151	4	4	4
Smart	Ima	101 Dummy Ave.	Arcadia	MI	40613	2	2	4
Green	Teeth	81 Brush Ct.	Millersville	PA	17603	1	0	1
Loser	Ima	12 Lost St.	Ephrata	PA	17651	0	0	1
Soul	Lost	0 Never St.	Somewhere	CO	80101	4	4	4

FIGURE 5-7

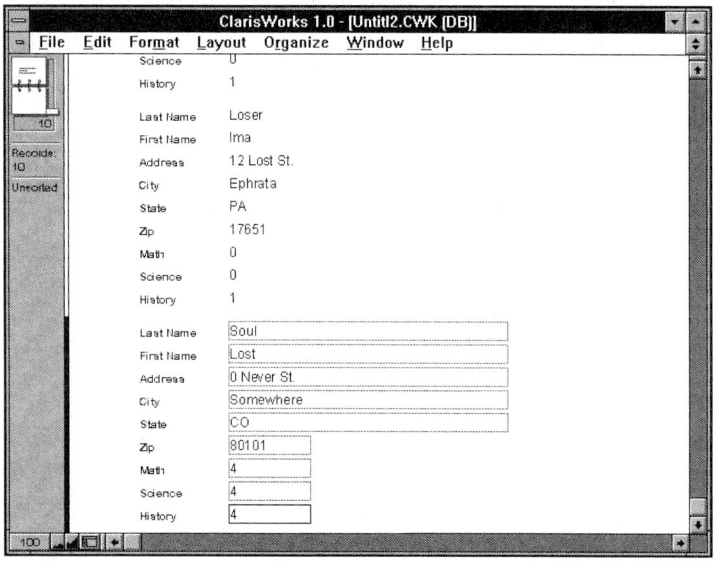

7. After creating a data file and entering some data, it is a good idea to save your document. Saving a document follows the same procedure as saving any other type of document in ClarisWorks. Save your document as FIRSTDB.CWK.

MODIFYING A DATA FILE

Several activities usually follow the creation of the initial structure of a database. If the planning was sound, then filling fields in records with data is the next step. However, if the planning process was poor, the database structure may need some modification. Usually, it is easier to change a database structure before entering any data into any record. However, that is not always possible. Many times users find the shortcomings of their database design only after entering large amounts of data.

If it is not possible to make changes before entering data, then it is critical to make changes as early in the data entry process as possible. The more data entered, the more difficult it is to avoid reentering large sets of data. The process of changing a database should follow as closely as possible the process of creating the initial data file structure.

Adding and removing fields to a data file begins by using the Define Fields option in the Layout menu. This produces the same dialog box used when the data file was first created. If you want to add a new field, simply type a new field name in the Name box and click on Create. If you want to delete a field, first click on the undesired field name, then click on Delete.

Adding fields does not automatically add data. When a new field is added to the data file, every record receives this new field—without data. Deleting records removes all data in every record residing in the deleted field. Therefore, be very careful about deleting fields, because you will delete not only the field name and type, but also any data associated with that field in every record in the data file.

CALCULATION AND SUMMARY FIELDS

Calculation and summary fields operate differently than any of the other four field types. With Calculation fields, data are automatically placed within the field of each record based on data entered into other fields. For example, a calculation field may be defined to produce an average of three number fields. You never enter data into a calculation field from the keyboard.

Calculation fields are very similar to formulas and functions used within a spreadsheet. When creating a calculation field, you follow the same steps used to create any other type of field. You must define both the field name and field type. However, when you've defined a field for calculation and click on Create, a new dialog box appears. This is the Enter Formula for Field dialog box. In this dialog box, you develop a formula by selecting from three columns of information—Fields, Operators, and Functions. For example, if you wanted to produce an average of three fields, you would first select AVERAGE from the list of functions, then select the three field names to average. If you wanted to add the contents of two fields, you would simply select one field name, followed by the addition operator (+), followed by the second field name.

Summary fields are similar to calculation fields. However, summary fields display totals and subtotals of data across records. Calculated fields base calculations on fields contained within one record. With summary fields, you may produce a Sub-Summary and Grand Summary for specific fields in sets or groups of records. For example, if you wanted to total all amounts paid on each record, you would use a Summary field.

Hands-On

1. Select Define Fields from the Layout menu.

   This produces the same Define Fields dialog box used to initially create the data file.

2. In the Name box, type **GPA** and select Calculation from the Type box. See Figure 5-8.

3. Click on Create.

   This produces the Enter Formula for Field "GPA" dialog box.

4. Select AVERAGE(number1,number2,...) from the list of Functions.

   This appears in the Formula box

5. Place the insertion point in front of *number1* within the parentheses.

6. Click on Math.

   This places the math field into the formula. Be sure to add a comma after the math field before adding the Science and History fields.

FIGURE 5-8

Define Fields	
Name	**Type**
Last Name	Text
First Name	Text
Address	Text
City	Text
State	Text
Zip	Number

Name: GPA

Type
- ◉ Text
- ○ Number
- ○ Date
- ○ Time
- ○ Calculation
- ○ Summary

Create Modify
Delete Done

7. Add Science and History to the list of fields.

Be sure there is a comma between each field name (except History) in the formula and delete any excess information, such as number1. See Figure 5-9.

8. Click on OK.

Notice that GPA is now added to the list of field definitions, and the formula used for the calculation appears under Type. See Figure 5-10.

9. Click on Done.

Each record now contains a GPA field with calculated data automatically placed in the field. Remember, it is not possible to directly add data to calculation fields.

10. Move through all records in this data file and notice the results.

FIGURE 5-9

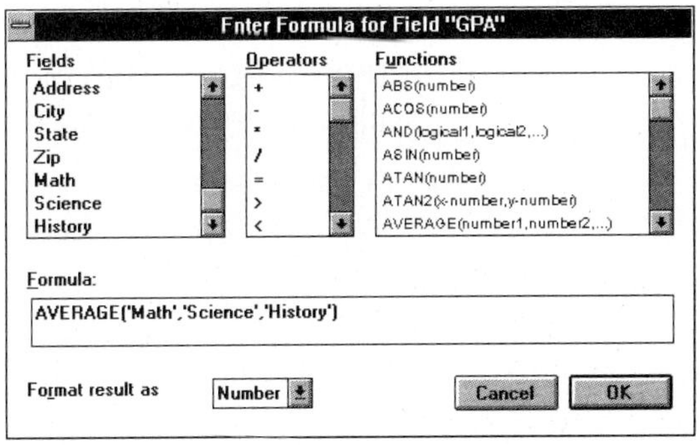

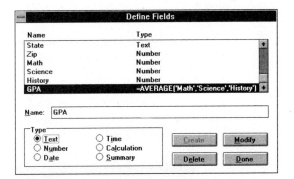

FIGURE 5-10

FINDING RECORDS

As the data file grows larger, it becomes more difficult to locate data by record number. Suppose you wanted to locate a specific record within the data file. If you knew the record number, you could use the Go To Record option in the Organize menu. However, if you did not know the record number you could locate a record through the Find option in the Layout menu.

Selecting the Find option in the Layout menu produces what appears to be an empty record. This is the Find screen, with which you may enter a search request. A search request entered into any field in the Find screen will cause ClarisWorks to locate only records that match the search request. For example, if you type Cold for Last Name, ClarisWorks will return all records that contain the data Cold in the Last Name field.

A search request may be based on one or more data fields. If you had 1,000 Smiths in your data file, you could include Smith for Last Name and Bob for the First Name. By including a second field, you limit the search.

ClarisWorks also provides the opportunity to locate multiple records based on operator searches. For example, you could enter <1/1/90 to return all records with a date prior to 1990. The search operators that are available include less than (<), greater than (>), less than or equal to (< =), greater than or equal to (> =), not equal (< >), and equal (=). Table 5-3 outlines a few examples.

Table 5-3 Search Options

Search Request	Located Records
= Smith	All records with Smith
< > Smith	All records except Smith
< 125	All records 124 and below
< = 125	All records 125 and below
> 6/1/94	All records after June 1, 1994
> = 6/1/94	All records after May 31, 1994

In addition to these operators, there are two special types of operators known as *logical* operators—AND and OR. Using AND allows you to further limit the scope of the search criteria. For example, if you want to locate all Smiths and Joneses in your data file, you could use the search criteria =SMITH OR =JONES. With AND, both expressions must be true to be available for a successful match. However, with OR, either expression can be available for a successful match. For example, with =SMITH AND =JONES, only records that have both Smith and Jones will be located.

Once you enter the search criteria in one or more fields, the next step is to click on Visible or All. All is selected to consider all records in the data file for the search request. Visible allows you to return only records that are currently available. If there are records in the data file you do not want included in a search, you may hide these records using the Hide Selected Records option from the

Organize menu. If this is the case with any record, you may select Visible from the Find screen. After selecting All or Visible, those records matching the search criteria are presented and ClarisWorks returns to Browse.

With the Find screen, you can also do multiple searches by establishing more than one search criteria. Begin by entering the first search criteria. However, before you click on Visible or All, select New Request from the Edit menu. This will give you a blank Find screen, on which you may develop your second search criteria. Only after you complete entering the search criteria should you select Visible or All to execute the multiple search criteria.

Hands-On

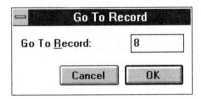

FIGURE 5-11

1. Select Go To Record from the Organize menu.

    Notice the dialog box, as shown in Figure 5-11.

2. Type **8**

3. Click on OK.

    Record number 8 appears onscreen.

4. Select the Find option from the Layout menu.

    Notice that the Find screen looks similar to the Browse screen. However, there is additional information under the Book.

5. For the Last Name field, type **Hot**

    See Figure 5-12.

6. Click on All.

    Only one record meets this search criteria.

FIGURE 5-12

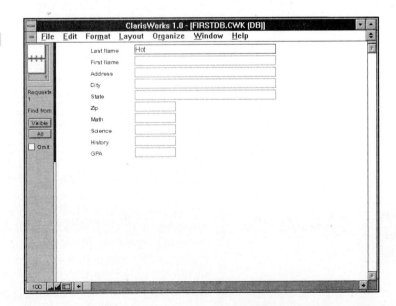

7. Select Find from the Layout menu.

8. For Last Name, type **< > Hot** and click on All.

Notice all records in the data file return, except record 2.

Exercise 5-2 Now that you know a bit about searching, it's time to practice. See if you can search based on the following criteria. Write down the number of records located from each search.

Locate all records from Colorado.

Locate all records except those from Pennsylvania.

Locate all records with GPA above 3.5.

Locate all records with GPA below 2.5.

Locate all records with GPA above 3 and a History grade above 3.

Experiment on your own.

SORTING RECORDS

In most cases, records are entered randomly. In other words, you seldom organize all data alphabetically before entering the data. But output from a data file usually requires the data be organized. For example, in finding multiple records, ClarisWorks will return these records based on record numbers. An alphabetic list of students is more useful than a random list.

ClarisWorks allows you to sort any type of data in ascending or descending order. In other words, you can produce a list with the most current date first or least current date first. You can produce a list from 10 to 1 or 1 to 10.

To begin a sort, select the Sort Records option in the Organize menu. This process brings up the Sort Records dialog box. There are two lists in this dialog box—Field List and Sort Order. You simply select the field on which you want to sort from the Field List, then click on Move to place the field name in the Order. You then select Ascending order or Descending order. If you want to sort on more than one field, you may add additional fields to the sort list. Typically, you would select Last Name as the first item in the sort order, then First Name as the second. This will sort the data file by last name. If there are two or more records with the same last name, they will be placed in order of First Name.

 *Hands-On*

1. Select Sort Records from the Organize menu.

Notice the Sort Records dialog box. See Figure 5-13.

2. Click on Last Name in the Field List.

Notice the Move button appears.

FIGURE 5-13

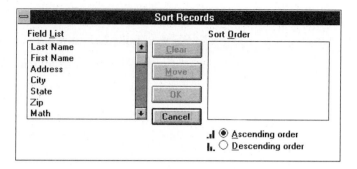

3. Click on Move.

    Last Name now appears as the first item in the Sort Order.

4. Be sure to select Ascending order.

5. Click on OK.

    Scroll through the records and notice the rearrangement of your data file. Be sure to notice that records now have new record numbers to reflect this new order.

Exercise 5-3   Change the order of records from best GPA to worst GPA. Who had the best? Who had the worst? Take several minutes to practice sorting on several different criteria. How would you sort your data file to produce a list of GPA from high to low that is alphabetized?

CUSTOM LAYOUTS

Up to this point, all work within the ClarisWorks database has used just one layout. But as mentioned at the beginning of this chapter, the layout is one of the two key components of any ClarisWorks database. The layout determines how data entered into the data file will appear both onscreen and on paper. Layouts are so important that once you start using this database, you are likely to build new layouts even before you enter any data into your data file.

Developing a new layout begins by selecting New Layout from the Layout menu. Each layout within the database must be given a unique name. This is the first piece of information in the New Layout dialog box. After giving the layout a new name, the next consideration is to determine the layout type. There are five types of layouts available—standard, duplicate, blank, columnar report, and labels, described in Table 5-4.

Table 5-4   Layout Types

Layouts	Description
Standard	Standard layouts contain all fields created for the data file. These are presented in order with each field on a separate line. The layout used in this chapter has been a standard layout.
Duplicate	Duplicate layouts create an exact duplicate of the current layout. In other words, it simply copies the current layout to a new layout name.
Blank	A blank layout is empty. This is used to customize a layout. You can select which fields, and in which order the fields will appear, in the layout.
Labels	The labels layout is used for creating mailing labels based on data within the data file. These are based on the types of labels that will be used during printing.

Since a data file can have more than one associated data file, it is quite common to create several layouts, each to accomplish a specific task within the database. For example, you may have a layout for entering data, another for listing results, another for generating mailing labels, and yet another for a separate set of calculations.

Blank Layouts

One of the most common layouts is Blank. It gives you the most flexibility in creating a new layout. When you select a Blank layout, the Browse screen returns without any field names. To add a field name to this layout, you must select Layout from the Layout menu, then select Insert Field from the Layout menu. This causes the field name and the box for entering data into this field to be placed in the Layout screen.

Both the field name and the field name box are components of this screen. Clicking on any component produces a series of boxes, or *handles*, indicating the component is active. You can move these components anywhere you want by clicking and dragging. Since the field name and the field name entry box are separate components, you can separate these onscreen. However, this is usually not a very good idea. You should keep the field name and the location where data will be entered into this field close together. You may also delete the component by activating it and pressing the del, delete, or backspace key.

In addition to moving and deleting components, you can change component attributes. For example, if you want to change the font and size of the field name, all you need do is first select the component, then choose any of the available format options from the Format menu. This includes Font, Size, Style, Alignment, and Spacing. These are the same format options available in other Claris-Works applications.

It is also possible to change the size of an attribute. For example, if you want less space for entering data, simply reduce the size of the box. This is accomplished by activating the component, then dragging any one of the four component handles.

By being able to customize a screen, you can determine the data entry order and which data to enter for which screen. The Layout option also allows you to add text and graphic lines to a layout. This is done by clicking on the A, or text tool, then placing the insertion point in the Layout screen and entering desired text. For example, if you want a title on each page, you may simply insert the text you want with its attributes. For titles, this must appear above the Body line. Field names and boxes should appear below the body line.

One of the advantages of Blank layouts is that you can produce a wide range of reports. For example, if you want a report that lists all students by GPA, you can develop a customized layout to use with printing or only for viewing data onscreen.

Hands-On

1. Select New Layout from the Layout menu.

2. Type **First Layout** for Name and select Blank from Type.

3. Click on OK.

   Notice the Layout screen. See Figure 5-14.

4. Click on the A in the tool bar to the left of the Layout screen.

   This produces the same I-beam used with word processing.

5. Click the I-beam above the Body line and type **School Grades**

   See Figure 5-15.

FIGURE 5-14

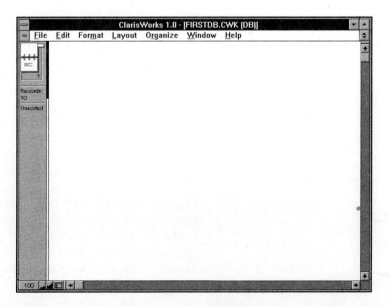

FIGURE 5-15

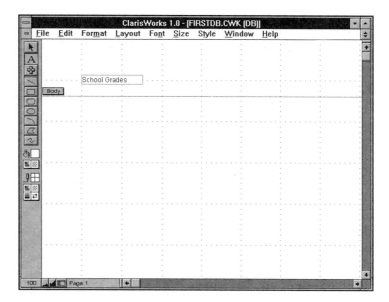

6. Click on the pointer tool to the left of the A, then point and click at the words *School Grades*.

   Notice that four handles appear, indicating that this box is active.

7. From the Format menu, set *School Grades* to use the Los Angeles font, 24 point, bold.

   Notice the text *School Grades* does not fit on one line.

8. Click and drag any of the handles to expand the box so that *School Grades* appears on one line. Then center *School Grades* in the middle of the Layout screen. See Figure 5-16.

FIGURE 5-16

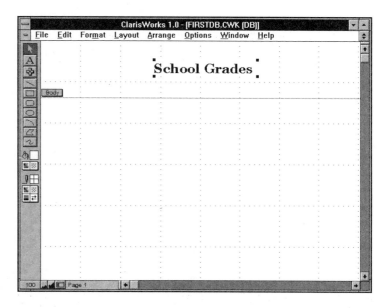

9. Select Insert Field from the Layout menu.

   This produces the Insert Field dialog box.

10. Click on First Name, then OK.

    Notice the field name and the location for entering data into this field appear on the Layout screen.

11. Click and drag the Body line near the bottom of the screen.

12. Click on First Name and drag the field title to the left, then drag the field entry box next to the field name.

13. Reduce the first name text entry box's size. See Figure 5-17.

14. Select Insert Field from the Layout menu, and select Last Name.

    Notice this field is added to the Layout screen.

15. Move the Last Name field so it appears to the right of First Name. Also, reduce the size of the data entry box. See Figure 5-18.

16. Design the rest of the layout to include Math, Science, History, and GPA. See Figure 5-19.

17. Select Browse from the Layout menu.

    Notice that the Browse screen now uses the newly created Layout.

18. If the records are spaced too far apart, return to the Layout option in the Layout menu and move the Body line up to a more appropriate location.

FIGURE 5-17

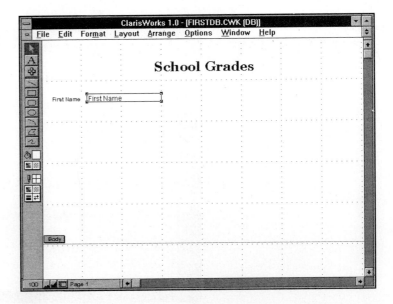

FIGURE 5-18

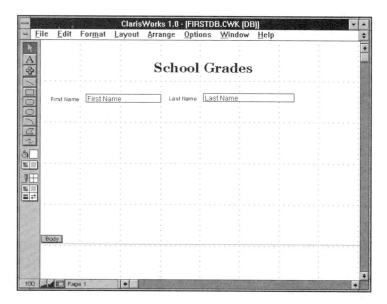

19. Select Layout 1 from the Layout menu.

Notice this returns the original standard layout.

20. Select First Layout to return to the newly-created layout.

You may select any layout at any time when working with a data file.

FIGURE 5-19

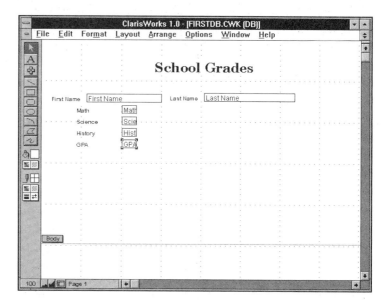

Exercise 5-4 You now know the very basics of creating a new layout. There are, however, many tools available for you to create highly appealing layouts. At this point, it is worthwhile to experiment. Try—create a new layout called Quick and use your imagination.

There are several graphics tools available. These can be employed when creating custom layouts. They will be discussed in the next chapter.

Columnar Report Layouts

Columnar layouts are very popular for producing data reports. With standard layouts, only a few records can be viewed onscreen at any one time. Also, when you print a standard layout, it uses a lot of paper. Columnar report layouts allow you to create a layout in which selected fields appear as columns, allowing a record to appear in a limited space.

The process for creating a columnar layout is much the same as creating any other type of layout. First, you must select New Layout from the Layout menu, then enter the layout name and type. Instead of viewing the standard layout screen, the Set Field Order dialog box appears. This dialog box allows you to select which fields will appear on the layout and in what order. This is the same type of dialog box used for sorting.

After selecting the fields you want to appear, clicking on OK produces the familiar Layout screen. On this screen, two areas exist— Header and Body. The header is used so the field names will appear once at the top of each page. Body includes the boxes for data from each field.

You can add additional text to the Header, such as a title, and you can adjust the width of any data entry boxes. In fact, you can manipulate the Columnar report layout in the same way as other layouts. However, it is a good idea to keep fields for each record on one line.

Hands-On

1. Select Layout from the Layout menu.

2. From the Layout menu, select New Layout.

3. From the New Layout dialog box, type **Grade List** for the layout name, select Columnar report for Type, and click on OK.

   Notice this produces the Set Field Order dialog box.

4. Under Field List, click on First Name, then on Move to place First Name in the Field Order.

5. Select Last Name and Move, then GPA and Move. See Figure 5-20.

FIGURE 5-20

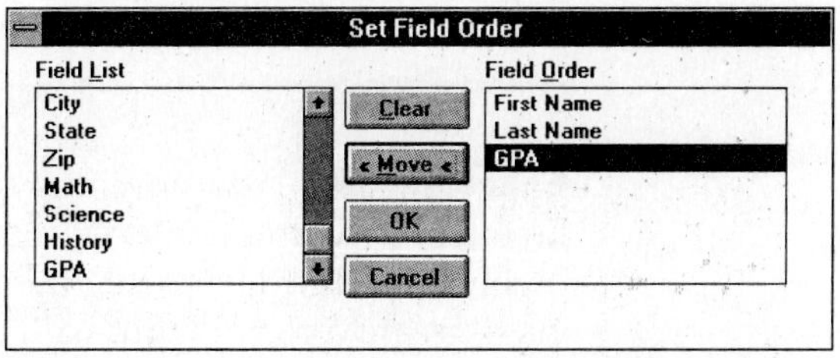

Set Field Order

Field List
City
State
Zip
Math
Science
History
GPA

Clear
‹ Move ‹
OK
Cancel

Field Order
First Name
Last Name
GPA

6. Click on OK.

    Notice in the Layout screen, the field names are above the field entry boxes. The field names also appear above the header line.

7. Reduce the field entry boxes so that they do not overlap. See Figure 5-21.

8. Above the field names, type the title **Semester Grades**.

    You will have to lower the Header line and the field titles.

9. Change the attributes to Roman, 24 point, bold, and center this title. See Figure 5-22.

10. Select Browse from the Layout menu.

    Notice the appearance of this new layout.

11. Select Print from the File menu to print a copy of this report.

FIGURE 5-21

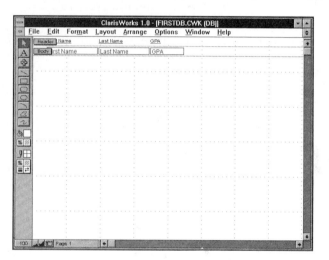

FIGURE 5-22

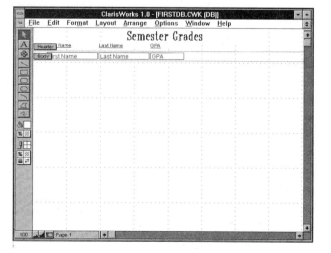

Exercise 5-5 Create a new columnar layout called All Grades. In this layout, create a report that will display all grades. Try to make this report as appealing as possible. You may want to use some graphic features to enhance the appeal of this layout. When you complete this assignment, be sure to print a copy of your report.

MAIL MERGE

One of the most popular uses of a database is to combine data from a data file with text generated in a word processor. Mail merge allows you to generate one letter in the word processor, then automatically address that letter to individuals found within a data file.

Mail merge combines a data file and a word processing file. Most of the work for mail merge occurs in the word processing document, based on data already established in the database document.

To mail merge, you must insert placeholders into your word processing document that match field names used within your database document. To insert a placeholder, select the Mail Merge option of the File menu in your word processing document. This allows you to select a data file, then causes the Mail Merge dialog box to appear. To insert a placeholder from this dialog box into your word processing document, select the desired Field Name, then click on Insert Field. This causes the placeholder to appear in your word processing document. Of course, this placeholder appears at the location of the insertion point.

If you want to print your word processing document linked to your database, you must use the Print Merge button in the Mail Merge dialog box. Clicking on this box prints as many copies of your word processing document as there are pieces of data in your database.

 *Hands-On*

1. Make sure you have saved your data file.
2. Select New from the File menu and select word processing.

   Notice both your database and word processing documents are available as a window.
3. Type the following letter. See Figure 5-23.

   Dear:

   This is to inform you your current GPA is.

   Respectfully,

   The Dean
4. Move the insertion point after Dear, insert a space, then select Mail Merge from the File menu.

FIGURE 5-23

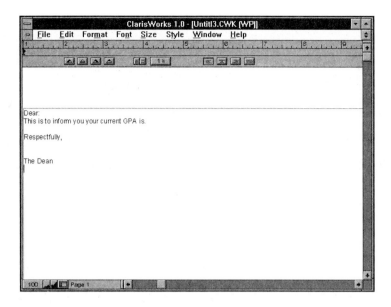

5. Select the FIRSTDB.CWK data file and click on OK.

Notice the Mail Merge dialog box, shown in Figure 5-24.

6. Click on First Name and Insert Field.

7. Click on the close box to end this dialog box.

Notice that <First Name> appears as part of the letter.

8. Click on the Control Menu box in the Mail Merge dialog box to return to the word processing document. Next, press the spacebar, then go back to Mail Merge and insert the Last Name field.

9. Add the necessary fields to this letter as depicted in Figure 5-25.

10. Once the word processing document is correct, select Print Merge and print your mail merged document.

11. Be sure to save this word processing document as FORMLTR.CWK.

FIGURE 5-24

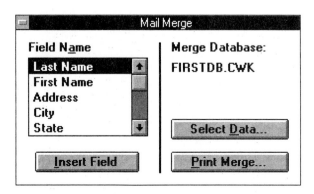

FIGURE 5-25

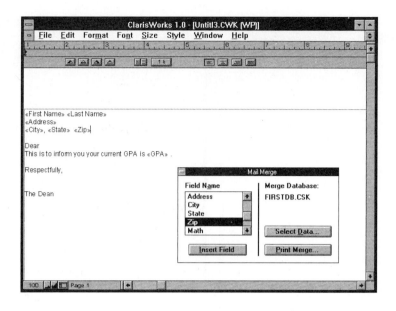

Summary

- Database software makes it possible for computers to store and retrieve large sets of data.

- The ClarisWorks database contains two primary components—a data file and a series of layouts.

- A data file is a document containing all data within the database.

- A layout is the mechanism for examining and manipulating the data file.

- Records are collections of data related to a single entity, such as a person or a place.

- A field is a specific location for the entry and storage of one set of data identified by field name.

- Naming is a very important aspect for data files, records, and fields.

- Field definitions require two factors—field name and field type.

- Text fields are for any type of data that you can type from the keyboard.

- Number fields are for numeric data that are available for mathematical computations.

- Date fields store date data.

■ Time fields store time data.

■ Calculation fields contain values derived from other data within the data file.

■ Summary fields are also based on data found with the data file.

■ Planning is the most important activity for successfully creating a usable database.

■ When you first create a data file, ClarisWorks automatically provides you with a layout.

■ To enter data from Browse, simply select the text entry box next to the desired field and type.

■ Adding fields does not automatically add data.

■ Deleting fields removes that field's data in every record.

■ A search request is that data entered into any field within the Find screen that will cause ClarisWorks to locate only records that match the search request.

■ A search request may be based on one or more data fields.

■ ClarisWorks allows you to sort any type of data in ascending or descending order.

■ By creating a customized screen, you can determine the data entry order and the data to enter for each screen.

■ Columnar layouts are very popular for producing data reports.

■ Mail merge allows you to generate one letter in the word processor, then automatically address that letter to individuals found within a data file.

Questions

1. In its simplest form, database software makes it possible for computers to _____ store _____ and _____ retrieve _____ large sets of data.

2. The ClarisWorks database contains two primary components— _____ Datafile _____ and a series of _____ layouts (How it appears) _____.

3. A _____ layout _____ is the mechanism for examining and manipulating the data file.

4. _____ Records _____ are collections of data related to a single entity, such as a person or a place.

5. A _____ field _____ is a specific location for the entry and storage of one set of data identified by field name.

6. When you create a data file in ClarisWorks, you must first specify each _____field_____ .

7. _____Text_____ fields are for any type of data that you can type from the keyboard.

8. A _____Search Request_____ is that data entered into any field within the Find screen that will cause ClarisWorks to locate only records that match the search request.

9. There are two special types of operators known as logical operators— _____and_____ and _____or_____ .

10. With the _____find_____ screen you can also do multiple searches by establishing more than one search criterion.

Quiz

1. Databases can store several types of data.
   - a. true
   - b. false

2. To store zip codes in a database, we must identify a zip code:
   - a. field
   - b. file
   - c. record
   - d. layout

3. To rearrange data by zip code is an example of:
   - a. a sort
   - b. search
   - c. find
   - d. inspection

4. A specific word used for searching fields is a:
   - a. search criterion
   - b. keyword
   - c. specificword
   - d. search word

5. Types of data stored in a field include text, number, date, time, summary, and:
   - a. columnar data
   - b. character data
   - c. calculation data
   - d. label data

6. A data file is a collection of records all made up of the same fields.
   - a. true
   - b. false

7. Mail Merge requires both:
   - a. word processing and spreadsheet documents
   - b. word processing and graphics documents
   - c. word processing and database documents
   - d. only word processing documents

8. Which of the following is not a type of layout?
   - a. standard
   - b. calculation
   - c. label
   - d. columnar report

9. It is possible to create a database without a layout.
   a. true   b. false

10. Only one search criterion may be specified for any data file.
    a. true   b. false

Applications

1. You have just been assigned to head a database development team designed to bring East Mudville Prep into the computer age. Your task is to develop a database that will enable the administrators and teachers at East Mudville to maintain student payment records. Create a new data file with the following field names and field types.

Field Name	Field Type
ID	Number
Last Name	Text
First Name	Text
Tuition	Number
Tuition Paid	Number
Balance	Calculation
Date Paid	Date

2. To the data file created for East Mudville Prep, add 20 students. You may make up any data that you want for each student.

3. Create a new layout for this data file that makes it easier to enter data. Call this layout *East Prep Entry*.

4. Create a new layout that will generate a report detailing all students who have not fully paid their tuition. Also, create a new layout that will generate a report detailing all students who paid prior to the beginning of school.

5. Create a report that details the total amount of tuition charged to all students, the total amount received from all students, and the total outstanding balance.

6

GRAPHICS ESSENTIALS

OBJECTIVES

Learning the material in this chapter will enable you to:

- distinguish between object-oriented and bit-mapped graphics
- create object-oriented graphics
- use various drawing tools for creating a graphic
- move, copy, and delete all or part of a graphic image
- use different fill and pen patterns
- rotate a selected portion of a graphic
- import graphics into documents created with the word processor

OVERVIEW

For those with little artistic ability and training, the thought of drawing a picture can be intimidating. But with a microcomputer and graphics software, even the most artistically challenged have the tools needed to create a variety of high-quality images. You need only supply a little imagination and a basic understanding of graphics software.

The graphics software provided with ClarisWorks performs many tasks that the unartistic find difficult to do by hand. Drawing a circle takes a steady hand, but with the graphics software in Claris-Works, drawing a circle is as easy as selecting a drawing tool and placing a circle onscreen.

Graphics software is also useful to the professional artist. ClarisWorks provides the professional artist with tools to create, edit, and produce high-quality designs. A graphic artist can easily create designs with the various drawing tools, change colors with a simple click of the mouse, and even resize and rotate the orientation of a graphic with simple menu selections—tasks as simple for the graphic artist as for the artistic novice.

This chapter provides an overview of the graphic capabilities found in ClarisWorks. As with the chapters on word processing, spreadsheets, and databases, learning to use the graphics applications within ClarisWorks requires a bit of practice and a lot of experimentation. This chapter will show you how to create graphics and will explain the graphic tools. However, it is up to you to experiment with these to fully understand how to create graphics.

TYPES OF GRAPHICS

There are two major types of graphics programs on the market today—draw programs and paint programs. While both of these programs allow you to create graphics, the process used for creating graphics is different. Both types of applications make it easy to create freehand drawings; however, the types of freehand drawings differ.

The drawing application is referred to as *draw-type* software. This type of graphic software uses objects placed onscreen to create images. Hence, these graphics are referred to as *object-oriented* graphics. With this type of software, selecting and using a tool creates a specific object, which becomes part of the overall graphic. For example, selecting a line tool allows you to create a single line object. Using the box tool allows you to create a box object. In object-oriented graphics, an object can be a line, a rectangle, square, circle, or any other object created with the tools provided with ClarisWorks.

To understand object-oriented graphics, consider a drawing of a kitchen table. As an object-oriented graphic, a kitchen table is made up of a rectangle representing the table top, sets of lines for each leg, and an oval for the base. Each shape or object remains independent of all other objects or shapes. The key point with object-oriented graphics is this independence. By being independent, each object may be moved or deleted without affecting other parts of the drawing.

Paint programs create graphics called paint-type graphics. Paint-type graphics do not treat additions to graphic images as independent objects. Rather, each time something is added to the graphic, the results become integrated into the total graphic. In other words, paint-type programs create graphics as complete entities.

Graphics produced with paint-type software are called *bit-mapped* graphics because each piece becomes part of the overall graphic design. The image generated is a collection of dots called *pixels.* With bit-mapped graphics, the image of a kitchen table is a single entity table rather than a group of individual objects. Therefore, once a leg is added to a table, it becomes a part of the entire table.

It is easy to see that object-oriented graphics (draw) provide much greater control and flexibility than bit-mapped graphics (paint). Object-oriented graphics use mathematical formulas to create independent images; these formulas allow each piece of the picture to be very exact and well-defined. Lines are smooth, crisp, and precise. On occasion, bit-mapped graphics appear jagged. On the other hand, since bit-mapped graphics are an integrated collection of dots, they allow for much greater detail. As a general rule, object-oriented graphics (draw) are preferable for line art and bit-mapped graphics (paint) are preferable for detailed pictures.

ClarisWorks for Windows graphics software is object-oriented. In other words, ClarisWorks is a draw-type program, not a paint program. All of the graphics created in ClarisWorks are objects that can be manipulated independently. Because ClarisWorks' is a draw program, you do have some limitations. For example, ClarisWorks' graphics software is not a good choice if you need to created detailed pictures. However, for most computer users, the draw program is both easy to use and provides the tools for most user-generated graphics.

DRAWING

Selecting Graphics from the New Document dialog box activates the drawing application. A document window appears, containing object-oriented tools and an area for creating the drawing object. The drawing area is filled with a grid of vertical and horizontal dotted lines. These lines are not part of the drawing, they are a tool to help you align objects. Along the left edge of the window are the tools available for creating objects.

When creating an object-oriented graphic, it is a good idea to turn on the ruler. The ruler can help you place objects precisely in the drawing area. If the rulers are not visible, select Show Rulers from the Window menu.

There are 12 tools for creating object-oriented graphics. Seven of these tools are for drawing. Figure 6-1 shows the drawing tools, the uses of which are summarized in Table 6-1.

FIGURE 6-1

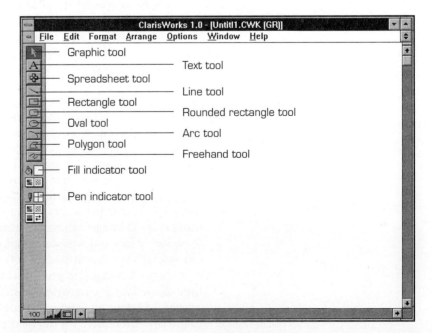

Table 6-1 Summary of Graphics Tools

Tools	Used to
Graphic Tool (Pointer)	Select objects to move, resize, or delete.
Text Tool	Draw a text frame for inserting text as an object.
Spreadsheet Tool	Draw a spreadsheet frame for creating a spreadsheet as part of the graphic.
Line Tool	Draw straight-line objects.
Rectangle Tool	Draw rectangular or square objects.
Rounded Rectangle Tool	Draw rectangles or square objects with rounded corners.
Oval Tool	Draw oval and circle objects.
Arc Tool	Draw arc and curved line objects.
Polygon Tool	Draw shapes with multiple angles and straight lines.
Freehand Tool	Draw irregular line objects.
Fill Indicator Tool	Fill an object with a color, pattern, or gradient.
Pen Indicator Tool	Set pen color, pattern, width, and arrow style for objects.

To use a tool, click on, or select, the desired tool. Once a tool is selected, the pointer changes to a unique shape representing the selected tool. To draw with a tool, place the tool anywhere in the drawing area, click and drag, then release. Clicking anchors the tool, dragging moves the tool, and releasing completes the object.

After drawing an object, it appears in the drawing area surrounded by handles (small black boxes). Drawing a line causes a handle to appear at each end of the line. Drawing a rectangle or oval causes four handles to appear—one in each corner. The handles are important because they indicate which object is selected and available for modification.

After drawing an object, the graphics tool (pointer) automatically returns. Only one object can be drawn each time you select a drawing tool. However, if you want to keep a tool active to draw several objects of the same type, double-click when selecting the tool. This locks the tool in place. Unlock a tool by selecting any other tool.

The next exercise takes you through the process of using each of the seven major drawing tools for creating objects. The remaining tools are discussed later in this chapter.

Hands-On

1. Start ClarisWorks.

2. From the New Document dialog box, click on Graphics, then on OK.

   This produces a screen with the drawing tools along the left edge of the window. The drawing area fills the rest of the window.

3. If the rulers are not visible in the drawing area, select Show Rulers from the Window menu.

4. Select the Line tool.

5. Place the Line tool pointer one inch from the left edge of the drawing area and one inch down.

   Notice that the pointer has changed to a cross-hair pointer.

6. Click and hold down the mouse button, then drag the cross-hair to the right two inches.

7. Release the mouse button.

   You have created a two-inch line object with two handles. The graphics tool automatically returns. See Figure 6-2.

8. Select the Rectangle tool and draw a one-inch square within the drawing area. See Figure 6-3.

   Four handles appear around this object.

9. Use the Rounded Rectangle tool to create a round-cornered one-inch square.

10. Use the Oval tool to create a one-inch circle.

FIGURE 6-2

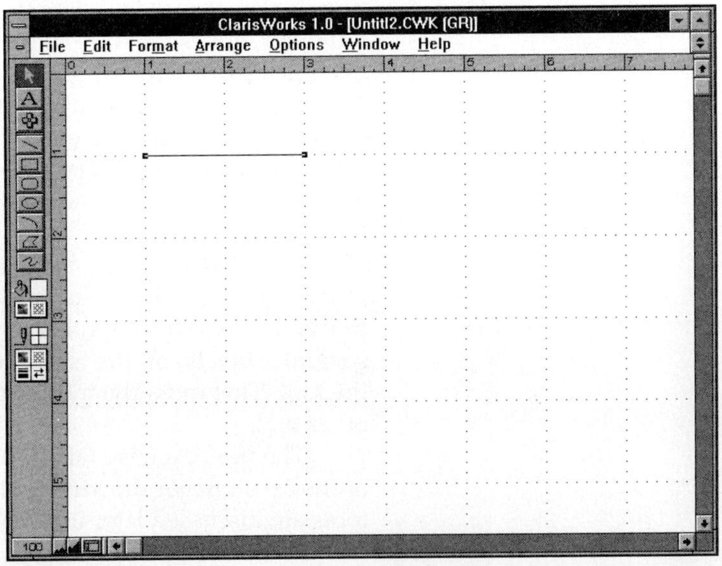

FIGURE 6-3

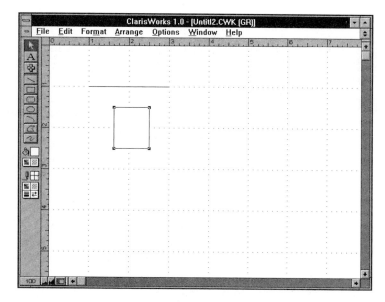

11. Use the Arc tool to create an arc within one grid line box.

12. With the Polygon tool, create a five-sided object within one grid line box. Click once to anchor, then draw one side and click again. This anchors the next side.

   Complete this process to create a polygon.

13. Use the Freehand tool to draw a "squiggly" line within one grid line box. See Figure 6-4.

FIGURE 6-4

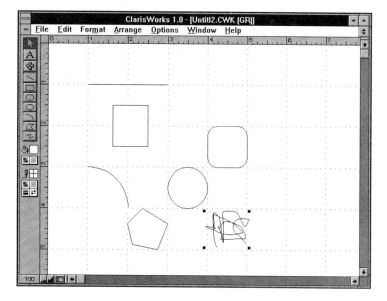

DELETING, MOVING, AND RESIZING OBJECTS

Very few people are able to create a perfect object on the first try. You will usually have to modify an object after placing it in the drawing area. Editing an object begins by selecting the object with the Graphics tool (pointer). You must select the Graphics tool, then click on the desired object. An object is selected, or active, when the handles appear.

To delete an object, first select it, then press the delete key. If you delete an object by mistake, use the Undo Clear option in the Edit menu to return the object. The Undo Clear option can bring a false sense of security; only the last deletion can be undone. Therefore, you must use the Undo Clear option before making further deletions.

To move an object to a new location within the drawing area, select the object, then click, hold, and drag the object to the new location. You can resize an object by clicking and dragging any of the object handles. Releasing the mouse button completes the resizing process.

Hands-On

1. Delete the square in your drawing area by first selecting the object with the Graphics tool then pressing Del or Backspace.

2. Select Undo Clear from the Edit menu.

    Notice that the square returns.

2. Expand the line to four inches in length by clicking on, dragging, then releasing the right handle.

3. Take all of the objects you created in the drawing area and use the resizing and moving options to create a meaningful image. Use your imagination and see what you can create. See Figure 6-5.

FIGURE 6-5

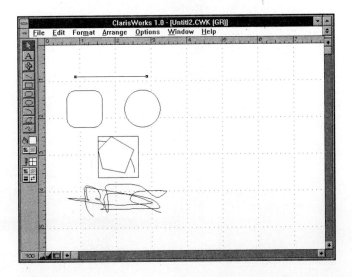

COPYING OBJECTS

You can make an exact duplicate of one or more objects by first selecting the object, then selecting the Copy option from the Edit menu. This puts the object in the clipboard. To place a duplicate of the object in the drawing area, use the Paste option from the Edit menu. Pasting an object within the same drawing area as the original causes the duplicate to appear on top of the original. Therefore, once you Paste, you need to move the duplicate off the original and to a new location within the drawing area.

1. Select the rounded rectangle object.

2. Select the Copy option from the Edit menu.

3. Select Paste from the Edit menu.

4. Click on the rounded rectangle in the drawing area and move this object one inch to the left.

   Notice the original remains in place and the copy moves to the new location. See Figure 6-6.

FIGURE 6-6

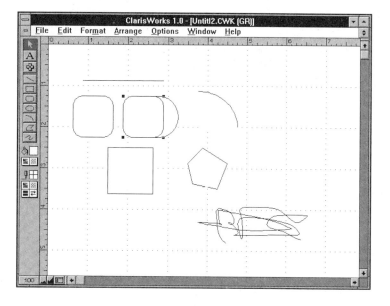

OBJECT ATTRIBUTES

To this point, all objects appear with the same line thickness and the same color. You can, of course, change any of these attributes in one of two ways. First, you may select an attribute prior to drawing the object. Second, you may change an attribute after the object appears on the drawing area. The two most common attributes are line and fill.

To fill an existing object, select the desired object, then select the Fill Indicator. The Fill Indicator consists of a Color Icon and the Pattern Icon. To select the Color or Pattern, click and hold. This causes all of the options for the icon to appear. While holding the mouse button, simply highlight any option, then release the mouse button. This causes the selected option to fill the object.

If you want to create an object with a specific fill, first select the desired tool, then select the desired fill. With both of these selected, you can create the object with the selected attributes. Once a fill attribute is selected, it appears in the Fill Indicator. This fill will remain in effect until changed.

The process for changing the pen attribute is similar to changing the fill. The only difference is that you must use the Pen Indicator. The Pen Indicator contains four icons—Color, Pen Width, Pattern, and Arrowhead.

The Color and Pattern icons are used the same as is the Fill Indicator. The Line icon allows you to select a line width. Several predefined widths are available. If you want a custom line width, the Other option allows you to specify any width. The Arrowhead icon allows you to place an arrow at one or both ends of a line.

1. Select the oval object in the drawing area.

2. Click and hold on the Pattern icon in the Fill Indicator.

   Notice the wide range of patterns that are available.

3. Select any pattern you desire and release the mouse button.

   The pattern fills the selected object. See Figure 6-7.

FIGURE 6-7

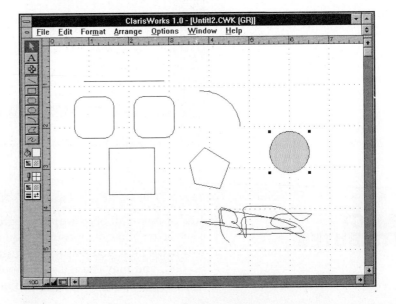

4. Select the Rectangle tool, then select a pattern from the Fill Indicator.

   Notice the pattern now appears within the Fill Indicator, as shown in Figure 6-8.

5. Create a one-inch square in the drawing area.

   Note that the square uses the selected fill.

6. Select the line in the drawing area.

7. Set the line width to six point, with arrows at both ends. See Figure 6-9.

8. Close this document and do not save. Be sure to do Exercise 6-1.

FIGURE 6-8

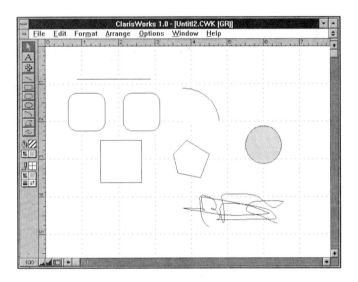

FIGURE 6-9

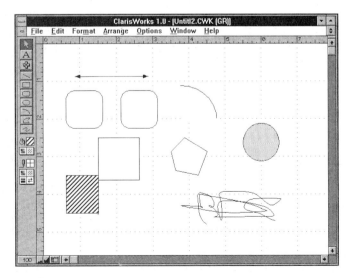

Exercise 6-1   Create a new drawing document. Draw a table. Be sure to save this document as TABLE.CWK on your disk and print a copy of your artwork.

TEXT AND SPREADSHEET OBJECTS

One of the big advantages of working with the drawing program within ClarisWorks is the ability to integrate text and spreadsheet objects into a drawing.

The Text tool allows you to create a text object to enter text in the drawing document. This is accomplished by selecting the Text tool, then creating a box in the drawing area. Once created, this box contains an insertion point for entering text. Text attribute options are similar to those found within the word processing program.

The Spreadsheet tool places a small worksheet in the drawing area. In the spreadsheet object, you can create a miniature version of a worksheet. As with text objects, you have many of the same controls of the spreadsheet object as within a spreadsheet document.

Once a text or spreadsheet object is created, it can be manipulated much the same as any other document. You can drag the object anywhere in the document, resize the object, and delete the object.

1. Using your table document, draw a text box on the table top.

2. Type **Table Top** in this text object.

3. Using the Text tool, select the text *Table Top* then choose Bookman, 18 point from the Format menu.

   Notice the text attributes change.

4. Label each of the other parts of the table. See Figure 6-10.

FIGURE 6-10

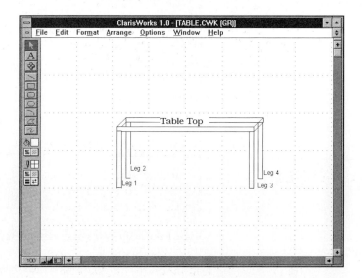

5   Use the Spreadsheet tool to create a worksheet within the drawing document.

6. With the Spreadsheet tool still selected, create the worksheet depicted in Figure 6-11.

7. Save your table document.

FIGURE 6-11

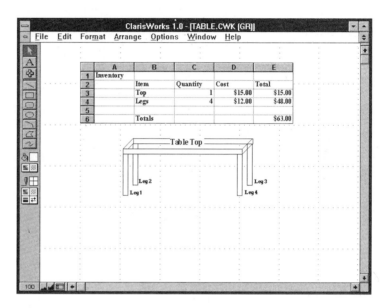

Exercise 6-2   Create a drawing of an organizational chart for a small business. You may want to include boxes for a Board of Directors, CEO, and several different departments. Make this drawing as visually appealing as possible. Save this as ORGCHRT.CWK on your disk and print a copy of your drawing.

Exercise 6-3   Time for more practice. Use the tools discussed so far to draw a house. Be as detailed as you like. Also, include your signature at the bottom of the painting. Save this document on your disk as HOUSE.CWK and print a copy.

SPECIAL EFFECTS

Selecting an object allows you access to options in the Arrange menu for altering an object and creating special effects. One of the most popular of these special effects is to rotate selected objects.

To rotate an object, select it and use the Flip Horizontal, Flip Vertical, or Rotate option. Flip Horizontal reverses the right and left sides of the selection. Flip Vertical puts the top on bottom and the bottom on top. Rotate turns the object 90 degrees.

You may also distort an object. This is accomplished by clicking and dragging any of the four handles. This will cause your object to reshape to fit the new dimensions as indicated by the handles.

1. Select one window in your HOUSE.CWK document created in Exercise 6-3.

2. Select the Flip Horizontal option in the Arrange menu.

   The image flips, as shown in Figure 6-12.

3. Leaving the same window selected, choose the Flip Vertical option.

   This turns the window upside down. See Figure 6-13.

FIGURE 6-12

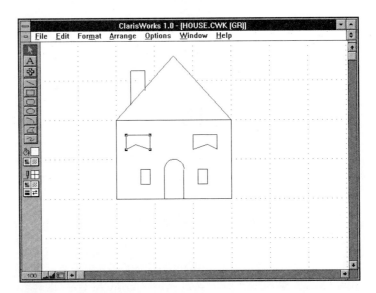

FIGURE 6-13

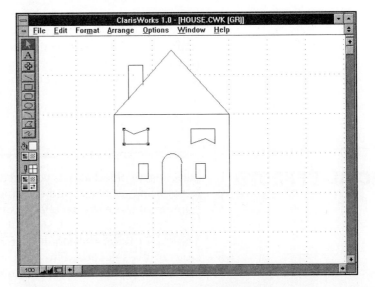

4. With the same window selected, choose the Rotate option in the Arrange menu.

   The window now appears on its side. See Figure 6-14.

5. Rotate the window back to its original position.

6. Select the window object.

7. Drag the upper right handle up and to the right about one-quarter inch, then release the mouse button.

   The image distorts to fill the area. See Figure 6-15.

FIGURE 6-14

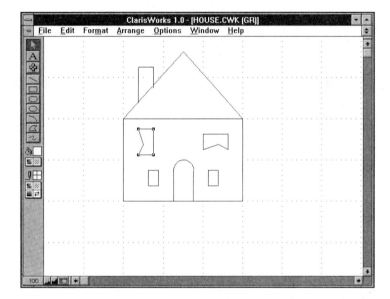

FIGURE 6-15

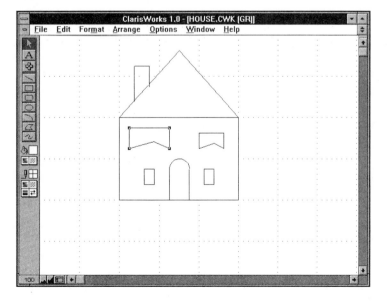

Exercise 6-4 More practice! Change the house so that the windows are distorted, the door is slanted, and the roof is rotated. Make any other change. Use the Save As option to save this new creation as HAUNTED.CWK.

DRAWING AND WORD PROCESSING

Graphic images can enhance your word processing document. Once you create and save a graphic on disk, you may then use that graphic within your word processing document (or any other Claris-Works document).

The process for inserting a graphic within a word processing document begins by first creating the desired graphic. The next step is to select all objects that make up the graphic. This is done by using the Select All option in the Edit menu. If you want only a portion of your graphic, you can use the graphic tool to select only the objects you want. By drawing a box completely around an object with the graphic tool, that object is selected. If the box is drawn around multiple objects, only objects contained wholly within that box are selected.

Once you select one or more objects, the next step is to use the Copy option in the Edit menu. This copies the object to the clipboard. Once the graphic is placed in the clipboard, simply open a word processing document and select Paste from the Edit menu.

The clipboard makes it easy to transfer all or some of any document to any other type of document. You can even copy a selection of text from a word processor to the clipboard, then Paste it in a graphic.

Hands-On

1. Close any existing documents and start a new graphic document.

2. Draw anything you like that can be used as a logo on letterhead stationery. Use your imagination to create a custom logo for yourself. See Figure 6-16.

3. Select your logo, then choose the Select All option, then the Copy option in the Edit menu. This places your logo on the clipboard.

4. Open a new word processing document.

5. Select the Paste option from the Edit menu of the word processing document.

   The logo appears within the word processor.

6. The logo within the word processor is treated as text. You may center your logo by selecting it, then selecting the center icon. Of course, you may make any other modification you desire.

7. Create the rest of your letterhead and save this as LTRHEAD.CWK on your disk. See Figure 6-17.

FIGURE 6-16

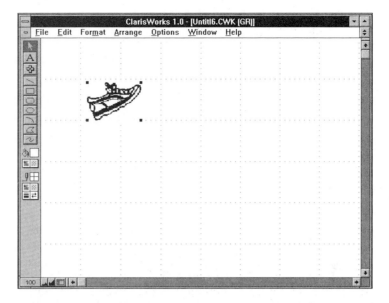

FIGURE 6-17

Summary

- ClarisWorks creates draw-type graphics.

- Draw software creates graphic objects known as object-oriented graphics.

- With draw software, each shape or object remains independent of all other objects or shapes.

- Object-oriented graphics use mathematical formulas to create independent images.

- When creating an object-oriented graphic, it is a good idea to turn on the ruler.

- The process of editing any object always begins by selecting the object with the Graphics tool to activate the object's handles.

- You may delete, copy, or paste any drawing object.

- The Fill Indicator consists of a Color Icon and Pattern Icon.

- The Pen Indicator contains four icons—Color, Pen Width, Pattern, and Arrowhead.

- The Text tool allows you to create a text object to enter text within the draw document.

- The Spreadsheet tool places a small worksheet within the drawing area.

- To rotate an object, first select it, then use either the Flip Horizontal, Flip Vertical, or Rotate option.

- Using the Clipboard, you can copy all or part of a graphic for use in any other ClarisWorks application.

Questions

1. In _____ graphics (the drawing application) an object can be a line, a rectangle, square, circle, or any other object created with the tools provided with ClarisWorks.

2. The key point with object-oriented graphics is _____ .

3. Graphics produced with paint-type software are called _____ graphics.

4. When creating an object-oriented graphic, it is a good idea to turn on the _____ .

5. Pasting an object within the same drawing area as the original causes the duplicate to appear _____ of the original.

6. The Fill Indicator consists of a _____ Icon and _____ Icon.

7. The _____ tool allows you to create a text object to enter text within the drawing document.

8. The _____ tool places a small worksheet within the drawing area.

9. When you select _____ from the _____ menu, a duplicate of the object moves to the clipboard.

10. The three options for rotating an object are _____ , _____ , and _____ .

Quiz

1. Which type of graphic software creates images mathematically?
    a. drawing   b. painting
    c. object-bit   d. none of the above

2. Which graphic tool is best for signing your name?
    a. Text tool   b. Freehand tool
    c. Pencil tool   d. Paint tool

3. Which tool is best for drawing a circle?
    a. Oval tool   b. Pencil tool
    c. Freehand tool   d. Arc tool

4. Which tool allows you to add color to a box?
    a. Fill Box tool   b. Fill Indicator tool
    c. Rectangle tool   d. Fill Rectangle tool

5. Which is best for drawing a triangle?
    a. Pencil tool   b. Polygon tool
    c. Regular Polygon tool   d. Triangle tool

6. Which tool changes the size of the drawing pen?
    a. Pencil tool   b. Pen Indicator tool
    c. Shape tool   d. Eyedropper tool

7. Which tool allows you to fill an area with a selected pattern?
    a. Spray Paint tool   b. Pencil tool
    c. Fill tool   d. Paint Pattern tool

8. Which tool allows you to create a circle?
    a. Line   b. Draw
    c. Oval   d. Circle

9. Which option allows to select every object within a drawing?
    a. Select Objects   b. Select All
    c. Select All Objects   d. Select Draw

10. Which option allows you to rotate an object 90 degrees?
    a. Flip Horizontal   b. Flip Vertical
    c. Rotate 90   d. Rotate

Applications

1. Design your own house. This design should include both the outside appearance and the inside floor plan. Be sure to save this graphic on your disk and print a copy.

2. Using the draw program, create your own personalized art to include on a letterhead. This may be a logo, a picture, or some other design. Be sure to save and print.

3. Design the cover page for a classroom newsletter. Include the name of the newsletter, and be sure to try different fonts and type sizes. Try a border around the edges of the page, experiment with different patterns in the border, and try different designs for the title. Experiment with as many Clarisworks features as possible.

4. Try to draw an object that has several intricate details. For example, try to draw a steam locomotive using a side view. Use a snapshot or picture from a book or magazine if necessary. Pay attention to the details. After drawing the object from a side view, try to create a graphic of the same device looking down on the object.

COMMUNICATION ESSENTIALS

OBJECTIVES

Learning the material in this chapter will enable you to:

- list the components of a telecommunications system
- describe how telecommunications software and modems work together
- describe the major controls of ClarisWorks communications
- describe the two major types of telecommunications
- describe byte length, stop bit, start bit, duplex, and parity
- describe the role of file transfer protocols
- describe the role of terminal emulation
- establish a communications setup with ClarisWorks

OVERVIEW

Imagine turning on your computer and having access to data stored in thousands of computers all across the country and even across the world. Access to these data would enable you to review news reports, financial data, scientific information, airline schedules, game software, and exchange electronic mail. This is the role of computer communication—to give you easy access to a world of information.

Computer communication is rapidly changing how we work. With computer communications, you can do library searches, locate bibliographic information, and play chess with others around the world, all from the comfort of your own computer. Computer communications has given new meaning to "going to work," because work can be anywhere there is a computer, a telephone, a modem, and the right kind of software.

What makes computer communications possible is the communications system. When one computer connects to another computer, it is the communications system that makes the transfer of data and information possible. Unlike the other types of software discussed in this book, communications is truly a *system*, rather than a discrete piece of software.

A communications system always consists of two components—hardware and software. Most often the system's hardware consists of a device that is able to send and receive data using telephone lines—the modem. The software side of the system controls the flow of information through the computer, to and from the modem. As part of the package, ClarisWorks provides software enabling you to use a modem to send and receive data. This is the communications software.

This chapter focuses on computer communications. It examines how modems work with the ClarisWorks communication software. This chapter also examines the methods for using ClarisWorks with modem to access information. Of course, you must have a modem, or this chapter will not have much meaning. If you do not, wait until you have access to a modem before working through this chapter.

COMMUNICATIONS

Telecommunications is the term used when computers communicate with each other using modems, telecommunications software, and existing telephone lines. This description is simple, but its application is far-reaching. Telecommunications allows anyone to access and exchange data with other computer users almost anywhere in the world.

The description of telecommunications includes a device called a modem (*mo*dulator-*dem*odulator). A modem connects the computer to the telephone lines. Its major function is to convert computer-generated data into a form usable by telephone lines (the modulate function), then change the data on the other end to a computer usable form (demodulate). Computers process data in a digital format. That is, all data in a computer are represented by a series of separate signals, zeros and ones. These signals are called *discrete* signals because each piece is separate from every other piece. Telephone lines, however, transmit data in the form of continuous waves called an *analog* format. Discrete signals cannot be sent on lines that require continuous waves. Modems convert digital signals to analog signals and analog signals to digital signals.

Communications software, such as that found within Claris-Works, controls both the modem and how data passes to and from the modem. In a communications system, both computers must have a modem, and both computers must have software to control the modem. But having the hardware and software is not enough. Both computers must agree on how data is exchanged. This is the function of the communications software.

There are several critical issues involved with successful telecommunications. For example, both computers must agree on the speed at which data is transmitted. If the sending computer sends faster than the receiving computer is able to receive, it is impossible to have a successful connection. Both computers must also agree on the language of the transmission, how they will encode and decode information. The following covers the most crucial concerns when connecting two computers together via telecommunications.

Selecting Baud

Controlling data transmission speed of the modem is a setting required for telecommunication software. Baud is the unit of measure for modem speed. Baud indicates bits per second (bps) of data transmission and reception. For example, 2,400 baud modems operate at 2,400 bps, or roughly 240 characters per second.

The most common modems operate at 300, 1,200, 2,400, and 9,600 baud. This baud rate corresponds to the maximum speed of the modem, which is preset and cannot be increased by the user. However, users can control modems to transmit data at slower speeds. For example, a 2,400 baud modem cannot operate at 4,800 baud, but a 2,400 baud modem can operate at 1,200 or 300 baud.

Both the sending and receiving modems must operate at the same baud rate. Therefore, the telecommunications software must be set by both users to match the baud rate of the connecting modem. If someone tries to send a document at 1,200 baud to a computer using a 300 baud modem, the data will not transfer. In this case, the person with the 1,200 baud modem must set the baud rate at 300 before transferring data.

Early modems used 300 baud or 30 characters per second, which by today's standard is very slow. The average person can read a page at about 45 characters per second. Think about how long it takes to read 100 pages of text. Sending a file that is 100 pages long can take a very long time at 300 baud. A 4,800 baud modem will send the same 100 pages 16 times faster.

Selecting Data Patterns

Before sending data between two modems, users must also agree on the pattern for sending the data. The two patterns are known as *asynchronous* and *synchronous* communications. In asynchronous communications, data is sent one byte at a time. A start bit indicates the beginning of each set of bytes, and a stop bit indicates the end. Asynchronous is the most popular form of communications. Synchronous communications does not use start and stop bits, nor send data in a series of bytes. Rather, synchronous communications sends information in a long string of bits. Synchronous communications is most frequently used by businesses or organizations that must transmit very large sets of data.

Most modems used with microcomputers use asynchronous communications for two reasons. First, telephone lines have a lot of static and interference, referred to as *noise*. Asynchronous communications sends one byte of data, then confirms that the byte received was actually the byte sent. Asynchronous communications is much more accommodating to noise because of this one byte-approach. Asynchronous communications also allows people to read information during transmission. In other words, the users of two computers connected with asynchronous modems can type messages back and forth. The major problem with asynchronous communications is slow speed. Synchronous transmissions send information in large groups of data, called *blocks*, at very fast speeds. These blocks are not readable until the completion of the entire transmission.

With asynchronous communications, users of both the sending and receiving computers must agree on three additional pieces of information before successful communication can occur. First, each user must determine how many bits make up a byte. This is called the byte length, word length, or character length. Seven- and eight-bit byte lengths are most common. Second, each user must specify how many stop bits, which indicate that a byte has been sent. Third, parity, or error-checking mechanisms, must be established. If a data service or the modem at the receiving end of a call specifies 2,400 baud with eight-bit byte length, one stop bit, and no parity, the calling telecommunications software must be set the same. In computer jargon, *8N1* represents eight-bit byte length, no parity, and one stop bit. Usually, this information is provided with a subscription to a service or is agreed to by computer users.

Setting Duplex

Duplex refers to the process or mode of sending data over telephone lines. With microcomputers, there are two duplex settings—full- and half-duplex. A modem sends a character, or a block of data, to another modem, then the receiving modem sends a signal back to verify the transfer. For half-duplex, data sends in only one direction. As with other settings, the telecommunications software of both the sending and receiving computers must use compatible duplex settings.

One indicator of the duplex setting is the screen display. If double characters appear on the screen, the duplex settings are not compatible. Similarly, if there are no characters visible on the screen, the user should change the duplex setting. Users must change the duplex setting in the telecommunications software to eliminate double characters or to see characters onscreen.

File Transfer Protocol

ClarisWorks supports a variety of procedures for sending entire data files with asynchronous communications. This is called a *file transfer protocol* because it determines the method for sending and receiving files. In short, a file transfer protocol is a procedure for sending error-free data from one computer to another.

There are a variety of procedures, or protocols, for transferring files to and from computers. No matter what the setting by the sending and receiving computers, both must use the same. Some communications programs provide their own unique file transfer procedures.

The process for using file transfer protocols begins with each computer user agreeing on the protocol. Typically, the sending computer reads a file from a disk and sends it to a modem. The receiving computer receives the file through the modem and sends it to be saved on a disk. The received file is exactly the same as the file originated by the other computer.

File transfers are only one method for receiving data. It is possible to capture non-file data as it is received. A capture buffer makes this possible. A capture buffer is an area of computer memory in which ClarisWorks stores incoming data. ClarisWorks turns on a capture buffer to capture all information sent, or the capture buffer can be toggled on and off to capture only selected pieces of data.

Setting Terminal Emulation

Using a modem to access a mainframe requires the connecting microcomputer to behave like one of the mainframe's terminals. Computer terminals are different from microcomputers. One difference is the structure and use of keys on the keyboard. For example, most terminals have a clear key. Most microcomputers do not. For a microcomputer to act like terminal, keys must be redefined to match the terminal requirements.

ClarisWorks provides several terminal options. This is necessary because different mainframes use different terminals to access data. For example, it is common for information services to require the use of a VT100. If a VT100 terminal is required, ClarisWorks must allow the connected computer to operate like a VT100. Usually, VT100 terminal emulation causes several keyboard keys to have new meanings.

THE TERMINAL PROGRAM

Selecting Communications from the New Document dialog box produces a document that is very different from any other created within ClarisWorks. The communications document does not have a tool bar, does not allow you to insert text or graphics, and does not allow you to create a document in the traditional sense. In fact, the communications program within ClarisWorks for Windows is not even a ClarisWorks program. ClarisWorks simply accesses the Terminal program found within Microsoft Windows. See Figure 7-1.

In communications jargon, the computer you connect to is referred to as the *host*, and the real goal of communication is to make your computer a terminal of the host computer. For this reason, it is up to you (the one who is calling the host) to make all necessary settings in the terminal program to match your modem to those of the host. This means you must set the baud rate according to the host. You must set the parity, the duplex, even the terminal emulation to match the requirements of the host computer.

FIGURE 7-1

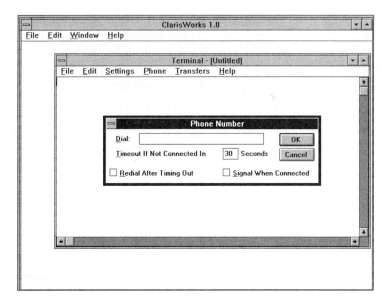

Creating a New Settings File

Communications with the Terminal program in Microsoft Windows begins by selecting Communications from the New Document dialog box. This invokes the Microsoft Windows Terminal program.

Within the Terminal program, you need to create a new settings file. This is done by specifying a series of communications settings, then saving these settings as a file. This allows you to create a number of settings files to communicate with different hosts. For each file, you need to specify the type of modem connected to your computer, where your modem is connected, and the settings required by the host.

The first setting you need to specify is through the Modem Commands option in the Settings menu. The Modem Commands dialog box will appear. In this dialog box, you need to insert all of the commands required by your modem. Different modems have different commands. Check your modem documentation to determine these settings.

In most cases, modems use one of three main modem defaults. For example, if your modem is Hayes-compatible, then all you need to do in this dialog box is select Hayes under Modem Defaults. This will cause command settings to adjust. If you don't know what your modem settings should be, try the Hayes default. Most modems use this command structure.

Once you establish the modem compatibility, the next step is to set the Communication options by using the Communication option in the Settings menu. There are several important settings. Some indicate how your modem is connected to your computer. Others indicate requirements of the host.

In the Communications dialog box is the Connector option. This determines where your modem is physically connected to your computer. Typically, this is COM1, 2, 3, or 4. Set this option first. Next, specify the maximum baud rate of your modem and the data bits, stop bits, parity, and flow control dictated by the host. Be sure these are accurate for the host for which you are building the settings file. If not, you will not be able to make a proper connection. If you need to guess, the most popular setting is 2,400 baud, no parity, 8 data bits, 1 stop bit, and Xon/Xoff. However, it's better not to guess.

The next step is to set the phone number. This is accomplished with the Phone Number option in the Setting menu. With this dialog box, simply enter the phone number of the host.

The next group of settings is for file transfers. This is set with the Binary Transfers option in the Settings menu. These settings are important if you plan to send or receive a file with the host. As with other settings, the file transfer protocol must be the same as the host's. The Terminal program supports only two file transfer protocols—XModem and Kermit. XModem is the most popular.

The fifth major setting is Terminal Emulation. This setting allows you to select the type of terminal used by the host computer. As with other settings, your settings will depend on what is required by the host computer. As a general rule, VT100/ANSI is a very popular type of terminal, used with most mainframe computers.

You can adjust the terminal settings by using the Terminal Preferences option in the Settings menu. This dialog box allows you to determine a wide number of settings, depending on the requirements of the host. There is a very important setting in the selected emulation. It is the duplex setting. This is indicated by the Local Echo box. Selecting this places the emulation in full duplex. Leaving this box blank leaves the setting in half duplex. Again, this setting is dictated by the host. However, if you are unable to see characters that you type onscreen, then change this setting. If you see double characters, also change this setting.

Once you have made the necessary settings, the final step is to save these communications settings as a file. As with other documents, this should be saved on a disk. Each file is designed for a single host. You may use just one communications document to build files for all of the other hosts. As long as the settings are the same, you can base new files on other files. This way you do not have to repeatedly go through the process of setting up your modem, protocol, or emulation. This works only if you plan to use these settings for all of your calls.

 *Hands-On*

1. Select Communications from the New Document dialog box.

    This launches Windows' Terminal program. See Figure 7-2.

FIGURE 7-2

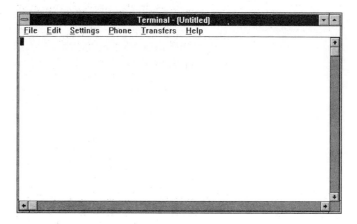

2. Select Modem Commands from the Settings menu.

   This produces the Modem Commands dialog box shown in Figure 7-3.

3. Set Command options according to your modem requirements. This information should be provided by your instructor.

4. Click on OK.

5. Select the Communications option from the Settings menu shown in Figure 7-4.

6. Select the Connector option first according to the requirements provided by your instructor.

7. Set Baud Rate, Data Bits, Stop Bits, Parity, and Flow Control according to the specifications of the host.

8. With all settings correct, click on OK.

9. Select Binary Transfers from the Settings menu.

   This produces the Binary Transfers dialog box, as shown in Figure 7-5.

10. Unless your instructor tells you otherwise, do not change any of these settings.

FIGURE 7-3

Modem Commands		
Commands	Prefix:	Suffix:
Dial:	ATDT	
Hangup:	+++	ATH
Binary TX:		
Binary RX:		
Originate:	ATQ0V1E1S0=0	

OK

Cancel

Modem Defaults
- ● Hayes
- ○ MultiTech
- ○ TrailBlazer
- ○ None

FIGURE 7-4

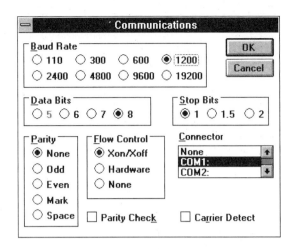

11. Select Terminal Emulation from the Settings menu.

    This produces the Terminal Emulation dialog box. Unless you have reason to, leave the emulation set to VT100 and click on OK.

12. Select Terminal Preferences from the Settings menu.

    You'll see the Terminal Preferences dialog box. Unless you are directed otherwise by your instructor or the requirements of the host, do not change any of these settings. See Figure 7-6.

13. Select the Phone Number option from the Settings menu.

    Enter the phone number of the host. Be sure to include any prefixes required to use outside lines. See Figure 7-7.

14. Select Save from the File menu to save your communications document. Use the file name MAIN.TRM.

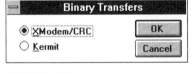

FIGURE 7-5

FIGURE 7-6

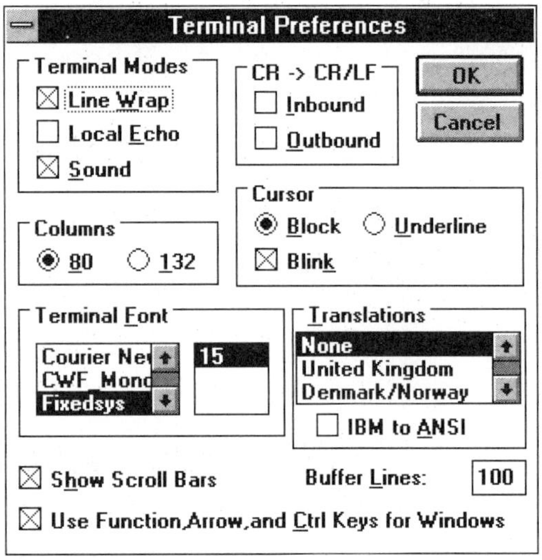

FIGURE 7-7

Phone Number

Dial: [   ]   [OK]

Timeout If Not Connected In   [30] Seconds   [Cancel]

☐ Redial After Timing Out   ☐ Signal When Connected

Placing a Call

Once you have set up your modem and established a communications file, the next step is to connect to a host. To connect to the host, make sure the modem is on, then select the Dial option in the Phone menu. This causes your modem to dial the phone number specified in the Phone Number option. The Terminal dialog box will indicate this. If your setup is correct, at this point your computer should be connected to the host. In most cases the host will then provide you with further instructions.

If you were unsuccessful at any point, you must verify that all settings are correct not only to your modem but to the requirements of the host.

Hands-On

1. Using the MAIN.TRM communication file, select the Dial option from the Phone menu.

   The Terminal dialog box appears. See Figure 7-8.

2. If all is successful, follow the instructions of the host computer and your instructor to telecommunicate.

FIGURE 7-8

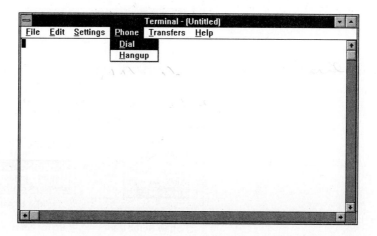

Sending and Receiving Files

One of the most important interactions between the Terminal program and the host occurs during file transfers. There are two types of transfers possible with the Terminal program—text and binary. Most users opt for binary because this allows you to send formatted files. In other words, with binary, you can send the files created with other ClarisWorks applications. Text files send text in a raw, unformatted fashion. Therefore, you should concentrate on binary transfers.

Binary transfers depend on the selected file transfer protocol. To send a file, you must tell the host to get ready to receive the file and the binary transfer format. In most cases, the host will prompt you for all the necessary information and even tell you when to start sending. As soon as the host informs you, you must select the Send Binary File option in the Transfers menu. This produces a dialog box in which you can specify both the location and file name to send. Clicking on OK allows host to start receiving the formatted file.

To receive a file from the host, you select the Receive Binary File option from the Transfer menu. As when sending, the host will prompt you when to make this selection. As soon as you select Receive Binary File, you should select both the location and name of the file you will be receiving. As soon as you click on OK, the host will start sending the specified formatted file.

Terminating

You can terminate any connection by selecting the Hangup option in the Phone menu. While you can disconnect your modem from the host at any time, it is a good idea to make sure you have followed the termination requirements of the host. In some cases, if you fail to exit the host correctly, you may have a difficult time reestablishing contact. Therefore, use the Hangup option with a bit of care.

Summary

- A communication system always consists of two components—hardware and software.

- A modem makes the connection between the computer and the telephone lines.

- Modems convert digital signals to analog signals (*modulator*) and analog signals to digital signals (*demodulator*).

- Baud is the unit of measure for modem speed.

- The two data patterns are known as asynchronous and synchronous communications.

- In asynchronous communications, data is sent one byte at a time.

- Synchronous communications does not use start and stop bits and does not send data in a series of bytes.

- In computer jargon, *8N1* represents eight-bit byte length, no parity, and one stop bit.

- Duplex refers to the process or mode of sending data over telephone lines.

- A file transfer protocol determines the method for sending and receiving files.

- In communications jargon, the computer you connect to is referred to as the host.

Questions

1. Telecommunications is the process by which computers communicate with each other by using _Modems_ , _Telecom software_ , and _____ .

2. Computer-generated data is in a _digital_ format, while telephone lines use an _analog_ format.

3. _Modems._ convert digital signals to analog signals and analog signals to digital signals.

4. _Baud_ is the unit of measure for modem speed.

5. The two data patterns are known as _Asynchronous_ and _Synchronous_ communications.

6. In _____ communications, data is sent one byte at a time.

7. In computer jargon, *8N1* represents _eight_ -bit byte length, _No_ parity, and _one_ stop-bit.

8. The file transfer _protocol_ determines the method for sending and receiving files.

9. There are two duplex settings— _full_ and _half_ .

10. The computer you connect to is called the _host_ .

Quiz

1. Any communication system is made up of what two components?
   - a. hardware and software
   - b. modem and emulator
   - c. software and telecommunications
   - d. telecommunications and terminal emulation

2. Which type of signal is used to carry information over telephone lines?
   - a. Analog
   - b. Digital
   - c. Baud
   - d. Duplex

3. Which type of data pattern sends one character at a time?
   - a. synchronous
   - b. asynchronous
   - c. multisynchronous
   - d. nonsynchronous

4. Which term indicates the speed of data transmission?
   - a. Bit
   - b. Baud
   - c. Byte
   - d. Asynchronous

5. Which term is associated with the way files transfer from one location to another?
   - a. protocol
   - b. multiplex
   - c. asynchronous
   - d. baud

6. Which of the following is not required for telecommunications?
   - a. modem
   - b. telephone line
   - c. communication software
   - d. printer

7. Both the sending computer and the receiving computer must use the same baud rate to communicate.
   - a. true
   - b. false

8. To make telecommunications work, connected computers must first agree on the number of bits per byte, the parity, and the stop bit.
   - a. true
   - b. false

9. The maximum speed of a modem can be increased by the user and software.
   - a. true
   - b. false

10. An area of computer memory where telecommunications stores incoming data is called a:
    - a. packed switch
    - b. VT100
    - c. capture buffer
    - d. terminal emulation

Applications

1. One of the most powerful applications of communications is through a communications network called Internet. Internet is a connection of computers located at universities, colleges, major libraries, even businesses. Through Internet, you can gain access to hundreds of computers. Check to see if Internet is available at your college or university. If it is, get access. The wealth of information available at little or, most often, no cost to you can be staggering.

2. Many communities have one or more local bulletin boards. Sometimes these are a bit hard to find. Ask your instructor, ask your computer center, ask even your local computer retailer if there is a local bulletin board, what the number is, and what the are the required communications settings. If you get this information, access this inexpensive source of information.

3. As you learn more about the types of information available, you may want to consider subscribing to one of the major communications services such as CompuServe, Prodigy, the Source, and others. There is a charge for this access. However, if you work at night and on the weekends, the costs are greatly reduced. Check with your local computer store for details on these and other services.

4. If you have a computer at home without a modem, buy one. Modems are no longer expensive additions. Rather, they are becoming a necessity. In fact, it does not make much sense to have a computer unless you have a modem.

ClarisWorks Commands

Add Field   To add a field to a database document, choose Layout from the Layout menu. Choose the layout desired, choose Insert Field, then select the name of the field to add. Click on OK.

Align Data   To align data in a spreadsheet, select the cells to align data, then select Alignment from the Format menu. Select General, Left, Center, or Right from the Alignment submenu.

Alignment   Select the desired text, then click on one of the alignment icons on the ruler.

Align Objects   Align graphic objects to each other by selecting the objects to align, then choosing Align Objects from the Arrange menu. In the Align Objects dialog box, select the Top to Bottom or Left to Right option. Click on OK. To align objects on the desktop, select objects to align, then choose Align to Grid from the Arrange menu.

Arc Angles   To change Arc Angles, select the arc to adjust, then choose Modify Arc from the Options menu. In the dialog box, enter the number for the start and arc angles. Click on OK.

Boldface   To boldface existing text, select the text, then choose Bold from the Style menu. To boldface new text, choose Bold and begin typing.

Calculate   To recalculate the spreadsheet automatically, choose AutoCalc from the Calculate menu.

Calculate Now   Choose Calculate Now from the Calculate menu to recalculate on demand.

Cell References   There are three types of cell references: absolute, relative, and mixed. The default cell reference in ClarisWorks is relative. Absolute references do not change when copying and pasting a formula; relative references change.

Charts   To create a spreadsheet chart, select the cells and choose Make Chart from the Options menu. Click on the chart type. To resume work on the spreadsheet, click on the spreadsheet.

Close   To leave a document and begin a new document, select Close from the File menu.

Columns   To create multiple columns in a text document, choose Columns from the Format menu. In the dialog box, type the number of columns desired, then enter the amount of space between columns. Click on OK.

Copy   To duplicate a block of text or data and maintain a copy in the original location, select text or cells, then select Copy from the Edit menu. Move the insertion point to the desired new location and select Paste from the Edit menu.

Cut   To move a block of text or data and delete it from the original location, select text or data, then select Cut from the Edit menu. Move the insertion point to the desired new location and select Paste from the Edit menu.

Define Field   To define a new field in a database document, choose Define Fields from the Layout menu. Type a field name and click on Field type in the Type area, then click on Create. When finished, click on Done.

Delete Cells   To delete a row or column of cells, select the row or column, then choose Delete Cells from the Calculate menu. To delete a range of cells, select the range of cells, then choose Delete Cells from the Calculate menu.

Delete Data   To delete a spreadsheet entry, select the cell to delete, then press Del or choose Clear from the Edit menu.

Delete Field   To delete a field, choose Define Fields from the Layout menu, select the name of the field to delete, and click on Delete. Click on OK to confirm the deletion. Click on Done when finished deleting fields.

Delete Record   To delete a record, select the record to be deleted, then choose Cut or Clear from the Edit menu.

Delete Text   Select the text to delete, then press [Backspace] or [Del], or choose Clear from the Edit menu.

Duplicate Layout   To design a new layout from an existing layout, choose the name of the layout to duplicate from the Layout menu. Choose New Layout from the Layout menu and type the name for the new layout in the New Layout dialog box. Click on Duplicate, then click OK.

Edit Data   To edit data in a cell, select the cell and retype the cell entry. Use the mouse to move the insertion point in the data and type an addition to the data.

Flip Objects   To flip an object, select the object to flip. Choose Flip Horizontal or Flip Vertical from the Arrange menu.

Font   To change a font for existing text, select the text, then choose a font from the Font menu. To change a font for new text, choose a font from the Font menu and begin typing.

Font Size   To change font size for existing text, select the text, then choose the size from the Size menu.

Formula   To enter a formula, select the cell, type an equal sign (=), then type the formula after the equal sign. Confirm the formula by clicking on the Accept button.

Function   To enter a function, place the insertion point on the desired cell, choose Paste Function from the Edit menu, select a function and click OK.

Hanging Indent   Select the paragraph, then hold down [Alt] and drag the left indent marker to the right.

Hide/Show Tools   Choose Hide or Show Tools from the Window menu.

Indent   To indent the first line of a paragraph, drag the first line indent marker away from the left margin.

Insert Date   Move the insertion point to desired location, then select Insert Date from the Edit menu.

Insert Time   Move the insertion point to the desired location, then select Insert Time from the Edit menu.

Italics   To italicize existing text, select text, then choose Italic from the Style menu. To italicize new text, choose Italic and begin typing.

Line Spacing   Default line spacing is set to single-spaced text. To change spacing for the entire document, choose Select All from the Edit menu. To change spacing for a paragraph, click on the paragraph so that it contains the insertion point, then click on the increase or decrease icon on the ruler.

Margins   To change the margin settings, choose Document from the Format menu and type the new margin widths in the margin boxes. Click on OK.

Move Object   To move an object, select the object and drag it to a new position.

Open Document   Choose Open from the File menu. Files with the ClarisWorks extension are listed in the File Name box for the directory selected. Choose a different directory or change the selection in the List Files of Type box.

Orientation   Change the print orientation with Print Setup from the File menu.

Page Break, Spreadsheet   Move the insertion point to the cell above and to the left of where the page break is to occur and choose Add Page Break from the Options menu.

Page Break, Text   Move the insertion point to the desired location, then select Insert Break from the Format menu or press [Enter] on the numeric keypad.

Page Numbers   Choose Insert Header or Insert Footer from the Format menu. If desired, type the word *Page* and include a space. Choose Insert Page # from the Edit menu.

Print   Select Print from the File menu.

Protect Cells   To protect cells, select the cells to be protected and choose Protect Cells from the Options menu.

Recalculate   To control when to recalculate a spreadsheet document, choose AutoCalc from the Calculate menu and remove the checkmark.

Redo   To reverse an Undo command, choose Redo from the Edit menu.

Resize Cells   To change the size of a row or column, select the row or column, then choose Column Width or Row Height from the Format menu. To change the size of all rows and columns, choose Select All from the Edit menu.

Resize Object   Select the object to resize and drag one of the handles in the desired direction. Press [Shift] and drag to resize proportionally.

Rotate   Rotate an object by selecting the object, then choosing Rotate from the Arrange menu.

Ruler   Hide or show the ruler by choosing Hide Rulers or Show Rulers from the Window menu.

Ruler Settings   To copy ruler settings to another paragraph, click on the paragraph with desired settings, Choose Copy Ruler, then click on the paragraph where the new settings are desired.

Save   Save a document by choosing Save from the File menu.

Save As   Save a document for the first time, or save an existing document with a new name by selecting Save As from the File menu.

Select Object   Select an object by clicking anywhere on the object. To select several objects, position the pointer at the beginning of a selection rectangle, and drag the rectangle until it encloses the objects to be selected. Holding down [Shift] and clicking will also select several objects.

Select Text   Select text by dragging the mouse pointer over the text. Select a word by double clicking on the word. Select a line by clicking three times rapidly on the line. Select a paragraph by clicking four times rapidly anywhere in the paragraph.

Sorting Cells   To sort cells, select the rows or columns to be sorted, choose Sort from the Calculate menu, and select a sort order.

Sorting Records   Choose Browse from the Layout menu, then choose Sort Records from the Organize menu. It may be necessary to use Show All Records from the Organize menu. In the Sort Records dialog box, select Ascending or Descending for the field name. With the field name still selected, click Move, then click Sort.

Spelling   To check the spelling in a document, choose Check Document from the Spelling submenu of the Edit menu. The spelling check begins at the insertion point in a text document. It begins at the first cell with a spreadsheet.

Tab Settings   Remove or delete a tab setting by dragging it off the ruler. To set a tab, drag the icon for type of tab to the desired position on the ruler.

Thesaurus   To find synonyms for a word, select Thesaurus from the Spelling submenu in the Edit menu.

Title Page   Create a title page by selecting Document from the Format menu, click on Title Page, then click on OK.

Undo   To undo a mistaken action immediately, choose Undo from the Edit menu.

Index